BENJAMIN FRANKLIN

1
A BOYHOOD IN BOSTON

The Franklins of Boston were poor, numerous, lively and intelligent. There were seventeen children in all, seven by their father's first wife, who had died after Josiah Franklin brought her from England to America; and ten by his second wife, Abiah, Benjamin's mother. Benjamin, born on January 6 (January 17, new style), 1706, was the youngest son, though he had two younger sisters, Jane, who was always his favorite, and Lydia.

They lived on Milk Street across from the Old South Church until he was six, when they took a larger house on Hanover Street. A blue ball hung over the door, serving to identify the house in lieu of street numbers. In June 1713, a firm of slave traders advertised "three able Negro men and three Negro women ... to be seen at the house of Mr. Josiah Franklin at the Blue Ball." Josiah kept no slaves himself but had a shed in which he allowed these captives to be housed.

Boston was then a busy seaport town, with some 12,000 population, next largest to Philadelphia in the American colonies. Its harbor was filled with sailing vessels; merchant ships from the Barbados or faraway England unloaded their goods at the Long Wharf. Streets were unpaved and unlighted, but there was plenty of activity in the coffeehouses and taverns. The town boasted of at least six book stores.

Benjamin could not remember when he learned to read. According to his sister Jane, he was reading the Bible at five and composing verses at seven. The verse writing was inspired by his father's brother, Uncle Benjamin, a versifier himself, who appeared at varying intervals, usually staying as long as his welcome lasted.

At a very young age, Benjamin devoured his father's religious tracts and sermons, but soon found boring their tirades against infidels and Catholics. *Pilgrim's Progress*, in contrast, was an absorbing adventure story, and *Plutarch's Lives* opened up a new and exciting world. His official schooling began at eight and lasted just two years. After that he worked in his father's soap and candle making shop, doing errands, dipping molds, cutting wick for candles.

With so many mouths to feed, higher education, such as that offered at nearby Harvard University, was out of reach for any of the Franklin children. To improve their minds, Josiah often invited men of learning to dinner, encouraging them to discuss worthwhile matters. Though his trade was lowly, he was one of the town's most respected citizens. Leading Bostonians often consulted him about public affairs, or asked him to arbitrate disputes. He was a man of many skills, was handy with tools, played the violin, and sang hymns in a pleasing voice. Benjamin's love of music began in his childhood.

The values of obedience and industry were implanted in all of them. "Seest thou a man diligent in his calling," Josiah would quote from Solomon, "he shall stand before kings, he shall not stand before mean men." Nothing then seemed more unlikely than that he, Benjamin Franklin, would ever stand before a king.

He was a sturdy, squarely built youngster, with a broad friendly face, light brown hair, and bright mischievous eyes. Among boys of his own age he was the leader— and sometimes led them into scrapes.

Once they were fishing for minnows in the salt marsh. Benjamin suggested they build a wharf so as not to get their feet wet. For the purpose, they appropriated a pile of stones belonging to some workmen who were using them to build a house. The wharf was a success but there were repercussions when the men found their stones missing.

"Nothing is useful which is not honest," Josiah told his erring son.

As a youth, he learned to handle boats, to swim, to dive, and to perform all manner of water stunts. One day he resolved to try swimming and flying his kite simultaneously. To his delight, he found that if he floated on his back while holding the kite's string, he was effortlessly drawn across the pond. Another time he carved himself two oval slabs of wood, shaped like a painter's palette, bored a hole for his thumb, and used them like oars to propel himself along. In this way he could easily outswim his comrades, though his wrists soon tired. He tried similar devices for his feet with less success. For this invention he might be called the first frog man.

He had no enthusiasm for cutting candle wicks and often dreamed of going to sea as an older brother had done. Josiah Franklin, sensing his discontent, told him he could take his pick of other trades. In turn, he took his son to watch the work of joiners, bricklayers, turners, and braziers. Young Benjamin admired the way they handled their tools but did not find these trades to his taste either.

Wisely, his father did not press him. His brother James had returned from England in 1717 with equipment to set up a printing shop at the corner of Queen Street and Dasset Alley. Since Benjamin liked to read, what would he think of being a printer—a trade that deals with pamphlets, books, everything made with words? The idea appealed to Benjamin, though he balked when he learned he would be apprenticed to his brother until he was twenty. His father insisted; the apprenticeship, legal as a slave contract, would assure him against losing a second son to the dangerous sea. When Benjamin finally signed the papers which bound him to his brother's service, he was twelve years old. Everyone agreed he was exceptionally bright for his age.

James Franklin was one of Boston's young intellectuals, belonging to what the pious Cotton Mather called the "Hell Fire Club," made up of clever young men like himself.

He had reason to be pleased with how quickly his little brother mastered the techniques of a printer's trade. As Benjamin's skill began to surpass his own, his attitude changed to resentment and jealousy. He found excuses to scold Benjamin, and sometimes gave him blows.

The shop handled pamphlets and advertisements and such odd jobs. As a sideline they printed patterns on linen, calico, and silk "in good figures, very lively and durable colours." In the second year of Benjamin's apprenticeship, their fortunes improved with a substantial contract to print the Boston *Gazette* for 40 weeks. The *Gazette* was one of Boston's two newspapers, both insufferably dull. When his contract came to an end, James decided to publish his own newspaper. His friends scoffed, saying that America had no need of still another newspaper!

The first issue of James Franklin's *New England Courant* appeared August 7, 1721, during a smallpox epidemic—and was devoted to opposing the new "doubtful and dangerous practice" of smallpox inoculation. There is no evidence that young Benjamin took any stand—either for or against—in the controversy.

The great advantage of working for his brother was that he had access to books. Several apprentices to booksellers with whom he made friends obligingly "loaned" him volumes from their masters' shelves. So they could be returned early in the morning before they were missed, he often sat up all night reading. There was also a tradesman named Matthew Adams with his own library, who took a fancy to Benjamin and let him borrow what he chose. From reading he turned his hand to writing, composing a ballad called *The Lighthouse Tragedy*, the account of the drowning of a ship's captain and his two daughters.

James saw possibilities in this effort, printed it for Benjamin, then sent him out on the streets to sell it. (The story of young Benjamin Franklin hawking his ballads on the streets of Boston would much later bring tears to the eyes of his aristocratic French friends.) *The Lighthouse Tragedy* was wonderfully popular, but his second ballad, a sailor's song about a pirate, was such a dismal failure that he allowed his father to discourage him from trying others.

"Verse-makers are usually beggars," Josiah Franklin had commented.

Prose was Benjamin's next effort. His inspiration was a volume of the London *Spectator*, with essays by Joseph Addison and Richard Steele, leading prose stylists of the eighteenth century. He made notes on their subject matter, laid the notes aside a few days, tried to reconstruct the original. He changed the essays into verse, endeavored to put them back to prose. Thus he strove to correct his own writing faults, on occasion having the thrill of finding he had in a phrase or expression improved the original.

Both reading and writing were done on his own time, before the shop opened in the morning, at night, and on Sundays when his conscience let him miss church. And still there were never enough hours in the day for all the learning he sought.

When he was sixteen he came under the influence of a book by a man named Tryon, who preached on the evils of eating "fish or flesh." He had been taking his dinners with James and the workmen at a boardinghouse run by a Mrs. Peabody. Would his brother agree to giving him half what he paid Mrs. Peabody and let him buy his own dinner? Benjamin proposed. James jumped at such a bargain. Henceforth the young apprentice dined on dried raisins and bread instead of roasts and legs of mutton. He even had money left over for books, and two extra hours in the empty shop to peruse them as he ate. One of the volumes he purchased at this time influenced him even more than Tryon and his vegetarianism.

This was Xenophon's *Memorabilia*, which told of Socrates and his philosophy.

Hitherto when Benjamin had an opinion, he stated it, as so many do, unequivocally as a fact. It had been a mystery to him why people so often took offense and set to arguing the opposite side of the question. Instead of saying outright what he had in mind, Socrates asked questions—and indirectly led people to his own opinion. From that time on, Benjamin used rarely such words as "certainly" or "undoubtedly," but expressed his own ideas with seeming diffidence and modesty. Rather than saying, "This is so," he substituted, "In my opinion, this might be so." He retained this habit of speech the rest of his life.

Outwardly more humble, he was inwardly gaining self-confidence. It seemed to him that the things which James and his literary friends wrote for the *Courant* were no better than he could do himself, but he was too smart to risk asking his brother to let him have an opportunity to try. One morning a letter was slipped under the door of the shop before any of the staff arrived. It was signed by a "Mrs. Silence Dogood."

Mrs. Dogood claimed to have been born on a ship bringing her parents from London to New England. Her father, so she said, was standing on the deck rejoicing at her birth when "a merciless wave" carried him to his death. In America, as soon as she was old enough, her hard-pressed mother had apprenticed her to a young country parson, whom the young girl later married. Now she was a widow with three children.

James printed Mrs. Dogood's first letter, as well as subsequent ones in which she expressed herself, wittily and clearly, on such varied subjects as the folly of fashionable dress, the character of the so-called weaker sex, the ill effects of liquor, the inferior quality of New England poetry, the need of insurance for widows and old maids, the hypocrisy of certain "pretenders to religion," and the uselessness of sending dullards to Harvard simply because their fathers could afford to pay their way.

Not until her column had become the most controversial and the most popular in the paper, did James Franklin learn that his apprentice-brother was Mrs. Dogood's creator.

In the meantime James was having his own troubles. Because of an editorial attack by one of his contributors on the Massachusetts governor, James was summoned before the City Council, sent to jail for a month, and released only when he agreed to make an abject apology. The City Council then forbade him to print or publish the *Courant*. In desperation, James and his friends hit on the scheme of making Benjamin, in name only, the *Courant* publisher. So it would be legal, James burned his brother's apprenticeship papers, although privately a new set was drawn up.

"Mrs. Dogood" added her voice to the indignation aroused at James Franklin's persecution. From the London *Journal*, she quoted an article: "Without Freedom of Thought, there can be no such Thing as Wisdom; and no such Thing as public liberty without Freedom of Speech." (Capitalization of nouns was then held part of elegant writing, a practice which Benjamin Franklin always followed carefully.)

He had a freer hand now and composed many articles for the *Courant*. At seventeen, he was without doubt the best writer in Boston, with a mind inferior to none. It is small wonder that his brother felt it his moral duty to exert his authority over him. There were arguments. There were more blows on the part of James.

Benjamin, by his own admission, was "perhaps ... too saucy and provoking."

One day he told his brother he was quitting. A runaway apprentice was subject to the same penalties as a runaway slave, but Benjamin's case was slightly different. James could not make public the secret apprenticeship papers without getting himself in trouble. He took out his fury by visiting other Boston printing shops to warn them not to employ his arrogant younger brother.

Benjamin resolved to go to New York. His only confidant was a young friend named Collins. Collins persuaded the captain of a New York sloop to give him passage, telling a fantastic yarn about Benjamin being pursued by a young woman who wanted to marry him. The captain would not have carried a runaway apprentice but goodnaturedly agreed to help the young "ne'er-do-well" elude the female sex.

New York, where Benjamin arrived after a three-day journey, had only 7,000 inhabitants but was suffused with an atmosphere of luxury unknown in Boston. Streets, paved with cobblestones, were filled with elegantly attired English officials and wealthy businessmen. Houses were mostly of brick with stairstep roofs in the Dutch style. Though the English had captured it from the Netherlands in 1674, Dutch customs still prevailed.

Benjamin called at once on William Bradford, New York's only printer. Bradford told him he needed no help—privately he thought the Boston youth unstable—but advised him to go to Philadelphia and see his son, Andrew Bradford, also a printer. He could guarantee nothing but at least there was no harm trying.

In history, William Bradford, a worthy man in his own way, has two indirect claims to fame. One was that a former apprentice of his named Peter Zenger braved official censure and served a prison sentence for the principle of freedom of the press. The other—that he refused a job to Benjamin Franklin.

2
A YOUNG MAN ON HIS OWN

No one could have looked sadder or funnier than Benjamin Franklin when he walked down Philadelphia's Market Street for the first time. At the Fourth Street intersection, a rosy-cheeked buxom young girl, standing in a doorway, burst out laughing at the sight of him. It was understandable. His traveling suit was wet, shrunken and shapeless. His pockets were bulging with spare socks and shirts. He was hugging a large puffy white roll tightly under each arm and simultaneously eating a third.

The journey from New York had been a series of mishaps. His ship nearly foundered in a squall off the Long Island coast and was becalmed near Block Island. Fresh water ran low. They would have gone hungry had not some of the passengers hauled in a batch of codfish. Benjamin found the aroma of frying fish so tempting that he there and then renounced Mr. Tryon's vegetarian regime, never returning to it except for lack of funds.

Thirty hours later they landed at Amboy, where a leaky ferry took him across to Perth Amboy. From there he walked some fifty miles to Burlington, a two-day hike in pouring rain, then caught a boat going down the Delaware. The captain was short a hand and Benjamin helped with the rowing.

By the time they reached Philadelphia, his entire fortune was a Dutch dollar and a shilling in copper. The captain told him he had earned his passage, but he insisted on paying the shilling. It was a matter of pride: "A man being sometimes more generous when he has but a little money than when he has plenty, perhaps thro' fear of being thought to have but little."

A three-penny piece had procured him the three enormous rolls. One of them satisfied his hunger. He gave the other two to a woman and child who had been on the boat with him. That night he slept at the Crooked Billet Tavern, to which a friendly Quaker directed him.

The next morning he made himself as presentable as he could and went to see Andrew Bradford, the printer. Young Bradford had no work but hospitably invited him to lodge with his family. The same day Benjamin called on another printer, Samuel Keimer, who promptly hired him. Thus within twenty-four hours of his inopportune arrival, he had a place to stay and a job.

Keimer was an eccentric little man with a long black beard who had but recently come from France. He was somewhat of a knave as Benjamin would learn later, and he knew little about his trade. His press was old and in disrepair with only one small and worn-out font (set of type). But the pay was good, or so it seemed to a youth who had never had a salary before. He soon had Keimer befuddled with admiration by quoting Socrates to him.

His employer was nervous about Benjamin living with a rival printer and in a few weeks arranged for him to lodge with a family named Read. His chest of clothes which he had shipped from New York had now arrived. When Keimer took him to his new landlady, Ben was dressed in his best, a handsome, husky well-mannered young man, about five feet ten inches, with a wide mouth and a humorous light in his brown eyes. He was introduced to the daughter of the house, Deborah Read. Both young people started in surprise. She was the same lass who had laughed at him as he walked down Market Street eating his roll.

Debby was a warmhearted outspoken young lady, cheerful and quite pretty. Although, unlike himself, she had little interest in improving her mind, he enjoyed her company. There was shortly some talk of marriage between them. Her parents discouraged the idea, saying they were both too young. Nor was Benjamin overly ardent in his courtship. He was not yet eighteen, and far too pleased to be free of family discipline to think of settling down as a married man.

Philadelphia was largely a Quaker town, with a sprinkling of Swedes and Finns and a large contingent of German immigrants. The rich farms surrounding it were cut into deep forests where Indians lingered. Bears and wolves were still shot at the city's gates. This "City of Brotherly Love" had been planned by William Penn, the noble Quaker to whom King Charles II had made a grant of the some forty thousand square miles of land that made up the province of Pennsylvania. In contrast to the royal colonies, like New York and Massachusetts, Pennsylvania was known as a "proprietary" colony.

At William Penn's death, his sons inherited the proprietorship. There was already some resentment because of the vast tracts which the Penns held tax-free.

In Philadelphia, Benjamin soon found friends of his own age and of kindred interests. There were three with whom he spent many social evenings: a pious young man named Watson, an argumentative one named Osborne, and

James Ralph, who fancied himself a poet. They exchanged ideas on a multitude of subjects and read each other things they had written. Franklin was not overworked on his job and had leisure for reading. His needs were few and he saved some money.

Certainly he missed his family but he dared not let them know where he was for fear of being dragged back to Boston. He did not realize that in the small and intimate world of the colonies news of a stranger was likely to get around. He had a brother-in-law, Robert Holmes, who was a sloop owner living in New Castle, forty miles from Philadelphia. Somehow Holmes learned of his whereabouts and wrote to tell him the worry he had caused his parents. Benjamin answered in considerable detail, explaining the reasons for his departure.

Soon afterwards two distinguished gentlemen knocked at Keimer's shop. Keimer spied them from an upstairs window. "Sir William Keith!" he gasped in awe, and rushed down the steps to open the door, bowing and scraping. Keith was governor of the province of Pennsylvania! With him was another important citizen, one Colonel French. No doubt Keimer expected some important commission. The governor, however, brushed him aside and demanded to see Mr. Benjamin Franklin.

"How do you do, sir," he said when Benjamin appeared. "I must reproach you for not making yourself known to me when you first arrived. I have heard fine things about you, very fine things indeed. The colonel and I are headed to the tavern across the way which serves an excellent Madeira. Would you care to join us?"

"I would be delighted, your honor," Benjamin told him, removing the leather apron which was a symbol of his trade. His face was as impassive as if it were an everyday occurrence to have a governor invite him for a glass of wine.

Keimer, mouth open, stared at them with the look of a "poisoned pig."

Over the Madeira, Benjamin learned that Keith knew Robert Holmes, his brother-in-law, and had seen his letter. Keith, a man of some literary pretensions himself, had been deeply impressed with his skill at expressing himself.

"The printers of Philadelphia are a wretched lot," Keith asserted. "From what your brother-in-law says, Mr. Franklin, I am convinced that you would succeed in your own shop. I will do all in my power to aid you."

As Benjamin basked in this heady tribute, the governor and Colonel French launched into ways and means of setting him up in the printing business. All that was needed was capital. Would not Benjamin's father provide the necessary backing? It was very unlikely, Benjamin commented.

"I will tell you what I will do," said the governor. "I will write to your father myself to tell him how much faith I have in your ability."

Dazzled, Benjamin agreed to make a trip home to deliver the governor's letter personally.

He took a leave of absence a few weeks later, telling Keimer only that he was visiting his family. A year before he had quit Boston, a near penniless runaway. He returned in triumph, wearing a new suit, carrying a watch, and jingling some five pounds of sterling in his pocket. His mother and father were overjoyed to see him, and his sisters crowded around him delightedly.

He could not resist going to the printing shop of his brother James. No doubt he strutted somewhat and bragged about his success. He showed the admiring workmen his silver money, a novelty in Boston where paper money was used, and handed each a piece of eight to buy a drink. Only James refused to be impressed. He grew increasingly glum during Benjamin's visit. Later he said Benjamin had gone out of his way to insult him and he would never forgive him.

That night Benjamin showed his father the letter from Sir William Keith. Josiah Franklin was pleased as any parent that such an important personage had taken an interest in his son but did not approve of Keith's proposal. In his opinion Benjamin was too young to have the responsibility of his own shop, he wrote in his politely worded reply.

"I see your father is a prudent man," Keith said later in Philadelphia when Benjamin came to make his report. He added that he had found there was a great difference in persons and that discretion did not always accompany years. Since Josiah Franklin did not recognize his son's unusual abilities, he, the governor, would sponsor him.

He had Benjamin regularly to his fine house for dinner the next weeks. Gradually he unfolded his plan. Benjamin must take his savings and go to England. There he could pick out for himself his own press, type fonts, paper, and whatever else he needed for a printing shop. The governor would provide him with letters of introduction and letters of credit to cover everything.

Who could have refused such a splendid opportunity? Toward the end of 1724, after quitting his employment with Keimer, Benjamin set sail for his first visit to the Old World. There had been a touching farewell to Deborah Read, to whom he promised to write often. James Ralph, his poet friend, went with him, having decided to try his fortune in England. Since the governor was busy with pressing affairs, Colonel French saw him off. He did not have the letters Keith had promised, but assured Benjamin they were safe in the captain's mailbag.

He had a pleasant trip and made one good friend—an elderly Quaker merchant named Thomas Denham. Not until they reached the English Channel did the ship captain sort out his mail. That was when

Benjamin learned that there were no letters of credit, no letters of introduction, nothing at all from Governor Keith. He was stranded in London, with only twelve pounds to his name.

In his bewilderment, he confided his plight to Denham.

"There is not the least probability that he wrote any letters for you," the Quaker told him. "No one who knows the governor would depend on him. As for his giving you any letters of credit—that is a sad joke. He has no credit to give."

"But why?" Benjamin asked. "Why would he play such a trick on me?"

"Do not think too harshly of him," Denham said charitably. "Keith wants to please everyone. Having little to give, he gives expectations."

It was a bitter lesson.

He stayed in London nearly eighteen months. It turned out to be as easy for him to find a job here as in Philadelphia. Part of the time he worked for a printer named Palmer and after that for a Mr. Watt. Under the tutelage of experienced workmen, he perfected his printing skills. He also attempted to improve his colleagues by urging them to drink water instead of beer for breakfast. The "Water American," they dubbed him, but a few of them followed his advice.

Not that he was a prude. London had much to offer a young man who was curious and alert and full of fun. There were operas in French or Italian, plays by William Shakespeare at the Drury Lane Theatre, scientific lectures, and the lure of dance halls. He wrote a pamphlet called "A Dissertation on Liberty and Necessity, Pleasure and Pain," which brought him some acclaim among London's young intellectuals. He presented an American curiosity, a purse of stone asbestos, to Sir Hans Sloane, secretary of the Royal Society, and almost met Sir Isaac Newton. James Ralph borrowed money from him and then split up with him without paying him back, in a quarrel over a pretty milliner. He sent off one letter to Deborah Read, but never got around to writing another.

He could not have missed observing the squalor of the slums and the contrasting elegance of the great lords with their postilions and liveried coachmen. That no such vast difference existed between rich and poor in America may have struck him, but he drew no moral lesson. He was not yet a crusader and his heart was set on having as good a time as his means allowed.

On occasion he went swimming in the Thames with a co-worker named Wygate, and once on an excursion to Chelsea he dazzled Wygate and his other companions with a display of the water exercises which he had invented in his childhood. A certain Sir William Wyndham, a friend of the great Jonathan Swift, heard of his prowess and invited him to teach swimming to his sons. About the same time, Wygate proposed that the two of them travel through Europe, earning their way as journeymen printers.

Both suggestions tempted Benjamin but he rejected them. His Quaker friend Thomas Denham had offered him a position in his Philadelphia importing company. Denham had made one fortune as a merchant and was set on making another. With the crying need of America's growing population for goods from abroad, there was no reason why he should not succeed. The salary was less than Franklin earned as a printer, but there would be handsome commissions, travel to foreign lands, and, so he believed, an assured future.

He set sail on July 23, 1726, on the *Berkshire*. It was October 11 before they reached Philadelphia. Franklin, now twenty, kept a journal on this long voyage. He had time to think, to observe nature, to philosophize.

An eclipse of the sun and one of the moon were notable events of the trip, duly recorded in his journal. The passengers fished for dolphins. He noted their glorious appearance in the water, their bodies "of a bright green, mixed with a silver colour, and their tails of a shining golden yellow," and wondered at the "vulgar error of the painters, who always represent this fish monstrously crooked and deformed."

From the Gulf Stream he fished out several branches of gulfweed and spent long hours studying a growth which he called "vegetable animals," resembling shellfish and yet seeming part of the weed. Noting a small crab of the same yellowish color as the weed, he deduced—erroneously but with logic—that the crab came from the "vegetable animals" as a butterfly comes from a cocoon.

The idiosyncrasies of his fellow passengers also came under his scrutiny. From watching the men play drafts he concluded that "if two persons equal in judgment play for a considerable sum, he that loves money will lose; his anxiety for the success of the game confounds him."

One of the passengers was caught cheating and would not pay a fine. The others refused to eat, drink or talk with him. The cheat soon paid up. "Man is a sociable being," young Franklin wrote in his journal, "and it is, for aught I know, one of the worst of punishments to be excluded from society."

He discovered that there was nothing like a contrary wind to bring out the worst in mankind: "... we grow sullen, silent, and reserved, and fret at each other upon every little occasion." At the sight of a ship from Dublin bound from New York, on the contrary, he commented: "There is something strangely cheering to the spirits in the meeting of a ship at sea ... after we had been long separated and excommunicated as it were from the rest of mankind."

Interesting as the trip was, there was no moment equal to that when one of the mess cried "Land! Land!" In less than an hour they perceived the tufts of trees. "I could not discern it so soon as the rest;

my eyes were dimmed with the suffusion of two small drops of joy."

He had set out to conquer Philadelphia three years before and had not succeeded. Now he was to have another try.

3
THE BIRTH OF POOR RICHARD

Deborah Read was married. This bit of news which greeted his return came as a shock, though he had only himself to blame. A luscious young woman like Debby could hardly be expected to nourish her affection on one letter in a year and a half.

He had, it seemed to him, three major causes for self-reproach in his past: the grief he had caused his parents by running away from Boston; the wrong he had done his brother James; and his long neglect of Debby. He resolved that henceforth his life would be conducted differently.

Printing was behind him now, or so he thought. Under Thomas Denham he set himself to learning the intricacies of merchandising. He lived with Denham; their relationship was that of father and son. It lasted only a few months. In February 1727, the good Quaker fell ill and did not recover. His executors took over his store, and Franklin was out of a job.

Swallowing his pride, he went back to Samuel Keimer. To his surprise his former employer welcomed him with open arms and even gave him a raise. He soon found out why. Keimer had hired half a dozen men at very low pay. The trouble was they knew nothing about printing. He needed Franklin to teach them their trade.

Obligingly, Franklin went to great pains to show the men everything he knew himself. He did considerably more than he was paid to do. When types wore out, instead of sending an order to England for more, he devised a copper mold to cast new type, the first time this had been done in America. He made their ink, and he started a sideline of engraving. All the techniques he had learned from the London experts, he now put to use.

Knowing Keimer, he did not expect gratitude nor did he get it. As business improved and as the workmen mastered their trade, the employer grew increasingly uncivil and quarrelsome. He complained that he was paying Franklin too much and nagged him incessantly. Matters soon came to a climax. One day Franklin heard a loud noise outside the shop and dashed to the window to see what was happening. He never did find out.

Keimer was standing in the street below and, on seeing Franklin's face at the window, he bawled him out in such violent and insulting terms that everyone in the neighborhood could hear. No job was worth that much. Franklin took his hat and walked out, never to come back.

That night a fellow journeyman named Hugh Meredith came to see him. Meredith, who had been a farmer and taken up printing only recently, was fed up with Keimer. He proposed that the two of them should go into partnership as soon as his period of service was up a few months hence. His father admired Franklin and was willing to finance them. Mr. Meredith senior soon confirmed the offer, privately telling Franklin he felt he would be a good influence on his son, who drank too much.

During the next months Franklin did odd jobs and, in his spare time, organized a club called the Junto. There were twelve members in all, including Hugh and two other printers, a shoemaker, a joiner, a scrivener, and others in modest trades. "The Leather Apron Club," the town's wealthier citizens nicknamed the Junto, because of the humble working class background of its membership.

The Junto met each Friday. Franklin provided them with a list of "queries" to be discussed. "Have you lately observed any encroachment on the just liberties of the people?" Already he was beginning to think in terms of civil rights. "Do you know of any deserving young beginner lately set up whom it lies in the power of the Junto any way to encourage?" He knew from personal experience how much it meant to a young man to have friends to give him support and advice. "Which is best: to make a friend of a wise and good man that is poor or of a rich man that is neither wise nor good?" His brief tussle with earning a living had convinced him that wisdom was preferable to riches.

"Whence comes the dew that stands on the outside of a tankard that has cold water in it in the summertime?" The latter was one of many scientific "queries" he suggested to the Junto, in line with his own curiosity about the mysteries of life.

To improve themselves, to cultivate ethical virtues, to lend a hand to their neighbors—all were included in the Junto's lofty aims. They composed essays on various subjects. If a member read something of interest in "history, morality, Poetry, physic, travels, mechanic arts," he shared his new knowledge with his fellow members.

They were not always serious. Sometimes they met for outdoor sports. They held banquets, composed and sang songs, made jokes, told stories, often had riotous times together. The friendships they formed were firm, lasting as long as they lived.

Occasionally Franklin caught sight of Sir William Keith on the street, The former governor would look uncomfortable and slink away. His fortune had deteriorated. Before very long, he fled to England, leaving his wife and daughter penniless; he died in a London debtors' prison.

In the spring of 1728, when Franklin was twenty-two, he and Hugh Meredith were ready to open their own printing shop in a house on High Street. Their first customer was a farmer who gave them five shillings to print an advertisement. No sum ever loomed so large.

Customers were few and far between those first months. It was not due to Franklin's partner that they survived at all. He was rarely sober enough to do a day's labor. His father had been optimistic in hoping that Franklin could change him. Eventually Hugh admitted that he would never make a printer.

"I was bred a farmer, Benjamin. 'Twas folly for me to come to town and apprentice myself to learn a new trade."

They talked the matter over and came to an agreement. Franklin would pay back Hugh's father the hundred pounds he had advanced for their printing equipment, pay Hugh's personal debts and give him thirty pounds and a new saddle. Two of his Junto friends loaned him the money he needed. Hugh took off for his farm, leaving Franklin, at twenty-three, the sole owner of the printing shop.

The common people of Pennsylvania at this time were pleading for paper money, such as was used in Massachusetts and other colonies, but the wealthier citizens opposed it. Franklin, siding with the people, wrote a pamphlet on "The Nature and Necessity of a Paper Currency," which he printed himself, and which swayed the Pennsylvania Assembly to pass a bill to issue such paper currency. For his contribution, Franklin was awarded the contract to print the money.

Soon afterward, Philadelphia's most esteemed lawyer, Andrew Hamilton, arranged for him to print the laws and votes of the government. Business was beginning to prosper.

With all orders he took infinite pains. He kept his equipment in excellent shape, cleaning the type himself. He used very white paper and very black inks and sometimes made decorative woodcuts to illustrate advertisements. He hired a workman and took an apprentice, but outworked them both, staying in the shop from dawn to near midnight.

His rival, Andrew Bradford, printed an address from the Pennsylvania Assembly to the governor in a slipshod manner. Franklin reprinted the same address elegantly, sending a copy to every Assembly member. The next year he was voted official printer for the Assembly. He started a stationer's shop to sell paper, booklets, and miscellaneous items. Perhaps to impress the citizens of Philadelphia with his industry, he carted his supplies from the wharf in a wheelbarrow, wearing his leather apron.

Philadelphia boasted only one newspaper, a dreary and conservative sheet which Bradford published. Franklin talked over with his friends his own desire to start a livelier paper. One of them betrayed him to Keimer, his other rival, who promptly put out a newspaper with the ambitious title, *The Universal Instructor in All Arts and Science, and Pennsylvania Gazette.*

That poor illiterate Keimer running a paper? It lasted only until September 1729 when Keimer, head over heels in debt, sold it to Franklin for a pittance and departed to the Barbados, never to return. The *Pennsylvania Gazette*, as he called it, became Franklin's newspaper to run as he wished.

That winter he performed his first scientific experiment, designed to find out if the heat of the sun was absorbed more readily by colored objects than by white ones. The experiment was so simple any child could do it; the wonder was no one had thought of it before. He took some tailor's samples—small squares of cloth in black, blue, green, purple, red, yellow, and white—and laid them out on the snow a bright sunny morning. In a few hours, the black square, which the sun had warmed most, had sunk low into the snow; the dark blue was almost as low; the other colors had sunk less deeply; while the white sample remained on the surface of the snow.

Franklin thought in terms of the practical value of this discovery: white clothes would be more suitable than black ones in a hot climate; summer hats should be white to repel the heat and prevent sunstroke; fruit walls, if painted black, could absorb enough of the sun's heat to stay warm at night, thereby helping to preserve the fruit from frost.

A glazier's family named Godfrey had been sharing his High Street house. He was lonely when they moved. Even his close friends of the Junto could not ease his longing to have a family of his own.

On occasion he visited the Read family. Deborah's marriage had turned out tragically. Her husband, a good workman but irresponsible, had, like Keimer, taken off to the West Indies to escape debts. Even worse, it turned out that he had a wife still living in England. Debby, who had come home to live with her mother, was so pale and sad Franklin was filled with pity for her. Perhaps first out of a desire to do good, Franklin did his best to cheer her up, and it pleased him no end to see the color gradually come back to her cheeks as her normally high spirits returned. No woman had ever appealed to him more than she. In time she responded to his affection. They were married on September 1, 1730.

Theirs was not the most romantic attachment in the world, but it endured.

"She proved a good and faithful helpmate," he wrote some years later in his *Autobiography*, "... we throve together, and have ever mutually endeavor'd to make each other happy." Indeed Debby proved the ideal wife for an ambitious young man. She helped him in his printing orders, by folding and stitching pamphlets or purchasing old linen rags for the paper makers, and she ran their stationer's shop. Since he preached the need of economy, she obligingly served him plain and simple fare and contented herself with the cheapest furniture. Nor did she complain when he went every Friday night to the meetings of the Junto.

The little club had now hired a hall for its weekly gatherings. As there was no good bookshop in Philadelphia, the members pooled their own books and loaned them to each other. This practice of communal sharing gave them so much pleasure that, at Franklin's suggestion, they commenced a public library. Every subscriber, Junto member or not, paid a sum down to buy books from England, and there was an annual contribution for additional purchases. America's earliest lending library had come into being, the first of many civic benefits which Franklin initiated over the years.

A rival organization to the Junto was the newly established Philadelphia branch of the Masons, mostly well-to-do citizens. The aim of Freemasonry was "to promote Friendship, mutual Assistance, and Good Fellowship." Franklin succeeded in becoming a member by a rather sly trick, a note in the *Gazette* claiming knowledge of the "Masonic mysteries." Since these "mysteries" were supposed to be highly secret, the members were so alarmed they invited the *Gazette's* editor and publisher to join their ranks. For many years he was a leader in Masonic affairs.

He had wanted to be a Mason, but no one could persuade him to join any church or denomination. That there was one God who made all things and that the soul was immortal, he believed firmly. He held that "the most acceptable service to God is doing good to man." Since all religious sects, in theory, preached the same, he never did see a reason to favor one of them above others.

Within a year or so of its inception, the *Pennsylvania Gazette* had the largest circulation of any paper in America. Profiting from the lessons he had learned while working for his brother James, he stressed human interest stories and local news. He ran an article on the harsh treatment of a ship captain to the Palatine immigrants. He published stories on robberies and murders, was not above poking fun at the stodgy official reports which filled the pages of Andrew Bradford's paper, and he took up the cudgel for the freedom of the press.

Most popular of all were his "Letters from the Readers," many of which he undoubtedly wrote himself. Thus "Anthony Afterwit" complained that his wife, who wished to play the grand lady, was ruining him. "Celia Single" scolded the *Gazette* editor for being partial to men. "Alice Addertongue," another contributor, announced the opening of her shop to sell "calumnies, slanders and other feminine wares." He ran advertisements, sometimes for runaway slaves (it would be some years before he crystallized his thinking on the evil of slavery), sometimes for a wife pleading to her husband to come home. He slipped in jokes as a good cook adds seasoning, and he refused to let the paper be used for personal quarrels.

In 1732, three years after launching the *Gazette*, he was ready for a new publishing venture, his celebrated *Poor Richard's Almanack*. There were other almanacs published in the colonies; almanacs in fact sold almost as well as Bibles. Soon *Poor Richard* eclipsed them all.

Like the others, it noted holidays, changes of season, dates of fairs, gave weather information, advised the best day to gather grapes or to sow seeds. Interspersed with such data were proverbs, verses, witticisms and epigrams, some original but a great many adapted from sayings of great writers of the past, trimmed to suit an American audience:

Light purse, heavy heart. A rich rogue is like a fat hog, who never does good till dead as a log. Eat to live, and not live to eat. Nothing more like a fool, than a drunken man. To lengthen thy life, lessen thy meals. None preaches better than the ant, and she says nothing. Observe all men; thyself most. Half the truth is often a great lie. Lost time is never found again. Little strokes, fell great oaks. Nothing but money is sweeter than honey. Love your enemies, for they tell you your faults. Love your neighbor; yet don't pull down your hedge. Don't throw stones at your neighbors', if your own windows are glass. The cat in gloves catches no mice. To err is human, to repent divine; to persist devilish. A brother may not be a friend, but a friend will always be a brother.

And, a tribute to Debby: "He that has not got a wife, is not yet a complete man."

Poor Richard had something to say on practically every subject under the sun. He was in turn witty, wise, and, in keeping with the time he lived in, somewhat bawdy. No matter that he was sometimes inconsistent and contradictory, that he might praise saving money at one moment and make fun of the miser the next. Americans—farmers, businessmen, wives and workmen—chuckled at him, laughed with him, and perhaps at times took his moral lessons to heart. Many of his maxims became embedded in the American language.

Because of *Poor Richard*, prosperity touched the family that had hitherto known only economy and hard work. One day Franklin came down to breakfast to find that Deborah had served his bread and milk not in his usual two-penny earthenware crock, but in a china bowl. Instead of his old pewter spoon, there was one of silver.

"What is the meaning of this, Debby?"

"My Pappy can afford a china bowl and a silver spoon now," she said.

4
THE CIVIC-MINDED CITIZEN

There were two children in the Franklin family now. The first was William, the other, Francis Folger, whom the father called Franky. He was proud of his sons. He had reason to want to be a good example to them.

One day he drew up a list of thirteen "virtues" as follows:

Temperance (eat not to dullness; drink not to elevation)

Silence (speak not but what may benefit others or yourself)

Order

Resolution (perform without fail what you resolve)

Frugality

Industry

Sincerity

Justice (wrong none by doing injuries)

Moderation

Cleanliness

Tranquillity

Chastity

Humility (imitate Jesus and Socrates)

Franklin's ambitious project was to try to achieve all these virtues, thus to approach as near as possible moral perfection. This was no New Year's Resolution to be lightly made and quickly forgotten. He purchased a small notebook, ruled the pages with red ink, making seven vertical columns, one for each day of the week, and thirteen horizontal columns, one for each virtue.

Each time he felt he had failed to practice one of his virtues he made a black mark in the proper square. Thus if he put a cross in the Tuesday column opposite Silence, he judged he had that day talked too much about trivial matters. The thirteenth virtue, Humility, suggested by a

Quaker friend, was a check on the others; if he was proud of his mastery over any of his virtues, he would be lacking in humility.

He kept this notebook regularly for a long time. The virtue which gave him most trouble was Order (let all your things have their places; let each part of your business have its time). Eventually he had to decide that he was not an orderly person and never would be. Nor did he ever claim that he achieved anywhere near "moral perfection" in any of the others, although he did give credit years later to his daily discipline for "the constant felicity of my life."

It is unlikely that in any other part of the world a grown and prospering businessman would have resolved to make himself more virtuous, with all the diligence of a schoolboy attacking a problem in arithmetic. His act was typically American. The colonies were young and growing and pliable, not old and set in their ways like the European nations. Young countries, like young people, harbor the seeds of idealism, yearnings for greatness, deep-rooted desires to be better in any or every sphere of activity than their predecessors or contemporaries. The youthful spirit that was part and parcel of America remained with Benjamin Franklin to the end of his days.

He was always trying to enlarge his mental horizons. For that aim he taught himself French, Italian, Spanish, and German, not yet dreaming that he would ever have practical use for these languages. He was at the same time widening his business activities, starting a branch of his printing shop in Charleston, South Carolina, on a partnership arrangement. It was the first of many branches.

In 1733, after an absence of ten years, he went back to Boston to see his family. His parents were well but there were some sad changes. Four of his sisters and one of his brothers had died. Jane, his beautiful young sister, closer to him than anyone else in the family, had been married for six years to a saddler named Edward Mecom, and had two boys, but her husband was in poor health and her children were also sickly. Tragedy had cast its first shadow over her. She would in the years to come lose her husband and twelve children, two of them dying insane, as the result of some unknown inherited sickness.

James was living in Newport, and on his way back to Philadelphia, Franklin paid this older brother a visit. Their reunion was cordial and old differences were ignored if not forgotten. James too was sick and knew that death was not far away. His former apprentice promised to take care of James' son and teach him the printing business. When James died two years later, Franklin sent the boy to school for five years and then took him into his home as an apprentice, thus making James "ample amends for the service I had depriv'd him of by leaving him so early."

All his life he would be giving aid—jobs, partnerships, loans, gifts and, less welcome, advice—to his family, his in-laws, his nieces, nephews, friends, and children of friends. The assistance was sometimes unappreciated and seldom rewarded. It played havoc with virtue number four, Frugality. Nor, as he had omitted the virtue of generosity from his list, did he ever give himself any good marks for such services.

Sorrow struck him personally on November 21, 1736, when Francis Folger, a grave and sweet-faced lad of four, died of smallpox. In the midst of his terrible grief, Franklin refuted a false rumor. It was not true, he wrote in the *Gazette*, that his boy had died as the result of smallpox inoculation. Had he been inoculated, his life might have been spared. He felt it important that his readers should know that he considered inoculation "a safe and beneficial practice."

The year of his son's death, he was appointed clerk to the Pennsylvania Assembly, and the following year he was made postmaster of Philadelphia. These were his first official positions, and there was pay and prestige attached to both. What matter if the Assembly sessions were so tedious he worked out mathematical puzzles to keep himself awake, and that his home on High Street now housed the city post office in addition to the Franklins, various relatives of both of them for varying lengths of times, servants, apprentices, and on occasion journeymen who had no other lodgings.

He had six of these workmen now, including a Swede and a German, which made it possible to print in those languages. They were all kept busy. He was public printer for Delaware, New Jersey and Maryland. Besides the *Almanack* and the *Gazette*, a number of books were coming off the High Street presses: Cato's *Moral Distichs; The Constitution of the Free-Masons*, the first Masonic book printed in America; Cadwallader Colden's *An Explication of the First Causes of Motion in Matter*; and Richardson's *Pamela*, the first novel printed in America.

Their stationer's shop now sold books as well as an astounding range of miscellany: goose quills, chocolate, cordials, cheese, codfish, compasses, scarlet broadcloth, four-wheeled chaises, Seneca rattlesnake root with directions on how to use it for pleurisy, ointments and salves for the "itch" and other ailments, made by the Widow Read, Debby's mother, and fine green Crown soap, unique in the colonies, produced by Franklin's brothers John and Peter who had learned the secret of its composition from their father.

In all this hustle and bustle, Franklin reigned as instigator and executor. He was a little heavier, his brown hair somewhat thinner, his face more mature, and his manner more calm and assured, but in his eyes was the same merriment of the Boston youth. Around the house and shop, he dressed in working clothes, red flannel shirt, leather breeches, and his old leather apron.

For meetings of the Masons or for dinners with prominent Philadelphians who were now demanding his company, he had more elegant attire. On such occasions he might wear his best black cloth breeches, velvet jacket, a Holland shirt with ruffles at the wrist and neck, calfskin shoes, high-quality worsted stockings, and a fashionable wig.

Debby never accompanied him to such affairs, nor would she have been comfortable if she had done so. The years of their marriage had put a wider social and intellectual gap between them. While Franklin had cultivated his mental powers and learned to speak as an equal to anyone, she was the same Debby he had married, grown older and plumper. Her voice was still rough, her language uncouth, her manners hearty, and her taste in clothes flamboyant. He never tried to change her. He appreciated her loyalty, her industry, her warm heart, and asked for nothing more. "My plain Country Joan," he called her in a ballad he wrote and sang for the members of the Junto:

> Of their Chloes and Phyllises poets may prate,
>
> I sing my plain Country Joan,
>
> These twelve years my wife, still the joy of my life,
>
> Blest day that I made her my own.

As for Debby, had anyone told her that her husband would one day be among the most famous men in the world, she would have laughed in his face. Not her "Pappy"—as she always called him. Not that he wasn't the best of husbands, a good provider, and really handy at doing things around the house.

She must have clapped her hands in delight at the stove he set up in their common room in 1740. Houses then were mostly heated by fireplaces. Large or small, they had in common that one was scorched on approaching the fire too closely and chilled at the far side of the room. It was impossible for a woman to sit by the window to sew on a winter day. Her fingers would be too stiff with cold to hold a needle. It was taken for granted that everyone had colds during the winter months, especially the women, who of necessity were indoors more than the men. There was the problem of smoke too. With the usual fireplace, most of the smoke came into the room instead of going up the chimney, blackening curtains and spreading soot everywhere.

Franklin's Pennsylvania Fireplace, later called the Franklin Stove, was made of cast iron, could be taken apart and moved easily from room to room. It spread no smoke and, most amazingly, heated the entire room an almost equal temperature.

Debby's sole complaint about her husband had to do with the way he spoiled his son William. Ever since the death of little Franky, he humored the boy to excess. William had a string of private schoolmasters—one of them decamped with Franklin's wardrobe when William was nine. He had his own pony, like the sons of the rich. Whatever the boy wanted, he managed to wangle from his indulgent father. "The greatest villain on earth," Debby once called this clever lad. The two of them never did get along.

Even William had to take second place after their first and only daughter, Sarah, was born in 1743. Sarah would bring to her father joy and comfort to modify the pain caused by his son.

He was busy that year with a new project. In May he issued a circular letter headed "Proposal for Promoting Useful Knowledge Among the British Plantations in North America," which be mailed to men of learning throughout the colonies. Now that the first drudgery of settling was over, he wrote, the time had come "to cultivate the finer arts and improve the common stock."

For this purpose, he proposed formation of an organization whose members, through meetings or by correspondence, would exchange information on all new scientific discoveries or inventions, and he offered his own services as secretary "till they shall be provided with one more capable." From this letter grew the American Philosophical Society, which came into being the following year. (The words "philosophical" and "scientific" were then used as synonyms.) Its activities were parallel to those of the famous Royal Society in London.

One of Franklin's first contributions to the new society was a paper on his "Pennsylvania Fireplace," which he and Debby had been enjoying several years, including diagrams and instructions on how to install it. He refused to patent his invention: "As we enjoy great advantages from the inventions of others, we should be glad of an opportunity to serve others by any invention of ours."

Also in 1743 he printed his "Proposal Relating to the Education of Youth in Pennsylvania," a pamphlet suggesting an academy of learning to match Yale, Harvard, and William and Mary College at Williamsburg. He launched this plan not as his own but as coming from some "public-spirited gentlemen," a tactical approach he had figured out to be more effective than using his own name.

The academy, he wrote, should be "not far from a river, having a garden, orchard, meadow, and a field or two." It should have a library. The students—youths from eight to sixteen—should "diet together plainly, temperately, and frugally." They should be trained in running, leaping, wrestling, and swimming.

Subjects studied should be "those things that are likely to be most useful and most ornamental." All should be taught to "write a fair hand" and to learn drawing, "a universal language, understood by all nations." They should learn grammar, with Addison, Pope, and Cato's *Letters* as models. He stressed the importance of elocution: "pronouncing properly, distinctly, emphatically." The curriculum should include mathematics, astronomy, history, geography, ancient customs, morality, but not Latin and Greek, unless a student had "an ardent desire to learn them."

Franklin's ideal and surprisingly modern academy was also to teach practical matters: invention, manufactures, trade, mechanics, "that art by which weak men perform such wonders ...," planting and grafting. There should be "now and then excursions made to the neighboring plantations of the best farmers, their methods observed and reasoned upon for the information of youth."

This "Proposal" was the genesis of the University of Pennsylvania, which in six years' time—1749—became a reality. (Franklin was elected first president, a post he held seven years.)

Philadelphia had as yet no regular police force. Its dark and narrow streets were in theory guarded by the local citizens, appointed in rotation by the ward constables. Often citizens preferred to pay the six shillings required to hire a substitute, money which might be dissipated in drink, leaving streets unguarded, or to pay the very ruffians against whom protection was needed. To abolish such abuses, Franklin persuaded his Junto members to campaign for a paid police force, which was voted a few years later.

Also through the Junto, he called public attention to Philadelphia's fire hazards and means of avoiding them. From this effort came the Union Fire Company, the first organized firemen in the colonies. Subsequently, he was responsible for the first fire insurance company in the colonies.

Since 1739, England had been at war with Spain, and in 1744, war with France erupted. The struggle involved the colonies when, in July 1747, French and Spanish privateers plundered two plantations on the Delaware River, a little below New Castle. There were rumors of a French plan to sack Philadelphia. The city had no defenses. The Quaker-dominated Assembly had refused to vote money for war purposes.

Seeing danger threaten, Franklin published "Plain Truth," a pamphlet which succeeded in convincing even the Quakers of the need for preparedness. Under his leadership, Pennsylvania's first volunteer militia, with some 10,000 members, was formed. He was offered the post of colonel in the Philadelphia branch. He declined, preferring to serve as a common soldier. William, now sixteen, was also in service, not in the militia but in a company raised by the British for a campaign against French Canada.

In 1748, France, Spain and England settled their difficulties temporarily in the peace treaty of Aix-la-Chapelle. For the time being, the colonies were free from danger of invasion or attack. At last the Franklin family could return to normal life.

He was forty-two and by the standards of the time a rich man. Since his income was sufficient for his needs, he made up his mind to retire. A fellow printer named David Hall took over the management of his printing shop. Franklin moved to a quiet part of town, at Race and Second streets, and bought a 300-acre farm in Burlington, New Jersey, where he could practice the art of a gentleman farmer.

It was time, he believed, to devote the remaining years of his life to his friends, to his writing, to the pursuit of learning. Particularly a branch of learning that had occupied his attention on and off for the past several years—the study of electricity.

5
THE THUNDER GIANT

A few years before his retirement, Franklin, on a visit to Boston, attended a display of electrical tricks given by a Dr. Adam Spencer of Scotland. There is no record of the nature of these "electrical tricks." Franklin commented later that Dr. Spencer was no expert and that they were imperfectly performed. Since he had never seen anything of the sort before, he was "surpris'd and pleased."

That sparks could be produced by friction had been known since ancient times. Little more was known about electricity until, in the first part of the eighteenth century, a young Frenchman, Charles François du Fay, identified two different types of electricity: *vitreous*, produced by rubbing glass with silk; *resinous*, produced by rubbing resin with wool or fur. Such frictional electricity was brief-lived. Sparks flashed and were gone, and that was the end of it.

Was there any way in which electric charges could be preserved from the rapid decay which they underwent in the air? Around 1747 two scientists were working independently on this problem— E. C. von Kleist of Pomerania and Pieter van Musschenbroek of the University of Leyden. Within a few months of each other, they had found a method of storing electricity in a container. The Leyden jar, this container was named. It was the first electrical condenser.

In one experiment Musschenbroek suspended a glass phial of water from a gun barrel by a wire which went down through a cork in the phial a few inches into the water. The gun barrel, hanging on a silk rope, had a metallic fringe inserted into the barrel which touched an electrically charged glass globe. A friend who was watching him, a man named Cunaeus, happened to grasp the phial with one hand and the wire with another. Immediately he felt a strange and startling sensation—reportedly the first manmade electric shock in history.

Musschenbroek repeated what Cunaeus had done, this time using a small glass bowl as his "Leyden jar." "I would not take a second shock for the King of France," he said.

Van Kleist in Pomerania produced the same effect. He lined the inside and outside of his Leyden jar with silver foil, charged the inner coat heavily, connected it with the outer foil by a wire which he held in his hand—and felt a violent shock run into his arm and chest.

A Leyden jar could take any number of forms. Even a wine bottle would serve. The type used most frequently during the next few years was a glass tube, some two and a half feet long, and just big enough around so that a man might grasp it easily in his hand. The advantage of this size and shape was that it could most conveniently be electrified, which was then done by hand, by rubbing the glass with a cloth or buckskin. This simple device gave impetus to research on electricity throughout Europe. It also provided a new form of entertainment.

Performers went from town to town with their Leyden jars, giving spectators the thrill of receiving electric shocks, and extolling the marvels of "electrical fire." Louis XV of France invited his guests to watch a novel spectacle arranged by his court philosopher, Abbé Jean-Antoine Nollet. The King's Guard in full uniform lined up before the throne, holding hands. The first one was instructed to grasp the wire or chain connected to the Leyden jar. They all jumped convulsively into the air as an electric current passed through them.

In Italy some scientists tried to cure paralysis by electric shock, claiming moderate success. In May 1748, for instance, Jean-François Calgagnia, thirty-five years old, was given an electric shock from a simple cylinder-type Leyden jar. Since the age of twelve, his left arm had been so paralyzed he could not lift his hand to his head. After the first electrical treatment he at once raised his arm and touched his face. There is no record as to whether the cure was permanent.

After Franklin became aware of this phenomenon, he was agog to try experiments on his own. He wrote of his interest to a London friend, Peter Collinson, a Quaker merchant and member of the Royal Society. Collinson promptly sent him a glass tube, along with suggestions as to how it might be used for electrical experiments. This was all Franklin needed to get started.

He was not trained in scientific matters as were many of his European contemporaries. He was unfamiliar with scientific jargon, and could only write about what he was doing in everyday language. But he had those qualities that are innate in any scientist, with or without a university degree—an inquiring mind, patience, and persistence.

His experiments, beginning with the winter of 1746, covered a wide range. He melted brass and steel needles by electricity, magnetized needles, fired dry gunpowder by an electric spark. He stripped the gilding from a book, and he electrified a small metallic crown above an engraving of the King of England—so that whoever touched the crown received a shock!

His home was soon so crowded with curious visitors trooping up and down the stairs, he could hardly get any work done. He solved the problem by having a glass blower make tubes similar to his, passing them out to friends so they could make their own experiments.

Several of the Junto members worked closely with him. At first they electrified the tube, as was still done in Europe, by vigorously rubbing one side of it with a piece of buckskin. One of the club members, a Silversmith named Philip Synge, devised a sort of grindstone, which revolved the tube as one turned a handle. To charge the tube with electricity, all that was needed was to hold the buckskin against the glass as it revolved, a vast saving in physical labor.

Another invention of Franklin and his associates was the first storage battery. For electrical plates they used eleven window glass panes about six by eight inches in size, covered with sheets of lead, and hung on silk cords by means of hooks of lead wire. They found it as easy to charge this "battery" with frictional electricity as to charge a single pane of glass.

Among his disciples was an unemployed Baptist minister named Ebenezer Kinnersley. Franklin suggested he might both serve science and earn his living if he held electrical demonstrations. Kinnersley's first announcement of a lecture, held in Newport, described "electrical fire" as having "an appearance like fishes swimming in the air," claiming this fire would "live in water, a river not being sufficient to quench the smallest spark of it." He promised his audience such wonders as "electrified money, which scarce anybody will take when offered ... a curious machine acting by means of electric fire, and playing a variety of tunes on eight musical bells ... the force of the electric spark, making a fair hole through a quire of paper...."

Kinnersley lectured in the colonies and the West Indies and was hugely successful. Neither he nor any of the other collaborators could rival Franklin's own achievements.

Early in 1747, he gave the names of positive and negative (or plus and minus) to the two types of electricity, to replace the unwieldy terms, resinous and vitreous. Positive and negative electricity became part of the scientific vocabulary. He was the first to refer to the *conductivity* of certain substances. Electricity passed easily through metals and water; they were *conductive*. Glass and wood were *nonconductive*, unless they were wet. He also noted that pointed metal rods were wonderfully effective "in drawing off and throwing off the electrical fire."

After he retired in 1748, he spent much more time on electricity. To Peter Collinson in London he wrote, "I never was before engaged in any study that so totally engrossed my attention and my time as this has lately done." He kept Collinson informed in detail of his experiments, not because he thought he had the final word but in the hope that his experiments might possibly prove helpful to English scientists.

It was to Collinson he described an electrical party to be held on the banks of the Schuylkill River in the spring of 1749: "A turkey is to be killed for our dinner by the electrical shock, and roasted by the electrical jack, before a fire kindled by the electrified bottle; when the healths of all the famous electricians in England, Holland, France, and Germany are to be drank in electrified bumpers, under the discharge of guns from an electrical battery."

For Christmas dinner that year, he started to electrocute another turkey, but inadvertently gave himself the shock intended for the fowl: "The company present ... say that the flash was very great and the crack as loud as a pistol.... I neither saw the one nor heard the other.... I then felt ... a universal blow throughout my whole body from head to foot.... That part of my hand and fingers which held the chain was left white, as though the blood had been driven out, and remained so eight or ten minutes after, feeling like dead flesh; and I had a numbness in my arms and the back of my neck which continued till the next morning but wore off."

He was apologetic rather than frightened by the near catastrophe, comparing himself to the Irishman "who, being about to steal powder, made a hole in the cask with a hot iron."

This was soon after he had come to the conclusion that what he now called "electrical fluid" had much in common with lightning—that indeed they might be one and the same thing. He was not the first to propose this theory but no one before him had been able to suggest how it might be tested.

Thunder and lightning had mystified humanity since the beginning of recorded history. The Greeks had held that thunderbolts were launched by the god Jupiter. (One Greek philosopher, Empedocles, thought that lightning was caused by the rays of the sun striking the clouds.) Hunters of primitive tribes prayed to the god of lightning, who was a killer, as they wished to be. Certain medicine men were said to be endowed with the gift of summoning lightning at will.

Since biblical days, lightning was assumed to be an act of heavenly vengeance, but no one could explain the paradox that it struck church steeples more frequently than other buildings. In medieval times, people believed that ringing church bells would keep lightning away, a belief that survived the death of countless unfortunate bell ringers.

About 1718, an English scientist, Jonathan Edwards, suggested that thunder and lightning might be produced by a "mighty fermentation, that is some way promoted by the cool moisture, and perhaps attraction of the clouds." There had been very few other attempts to give a scientific explanation of the phenomenon, and even in Franklin's time many preachers considered lightning a manifestation of the Divine Will.

"Electrical fluid" and lightning had in common, Franklin wrote in his notes on November 7, 1749, that they both gave light, had a crooked direction and swift motion, and were conducted by metals. Both melted metals and could destroy animals. Since they were similar in so many respects, would it not follow that lightning, like "electrical fluid" would be attracted by pointed rods? "Let the experiment be made."

By May 1750, he was sure enough of his hypothesis that he elaborated to Peter Collinson the advantages to humanity of what later were called lightning rods:

I am of the opinion that houses, ships, and even towers and churches may be effectually secured from the strokes of lightning ... if, instead of the round balls of wood or metal which are commonly placed on tops of weathercocks, vanes, or masts, there should be a rod of iron eight or ten feet in length, sharpened gradually to a point like a needle ... the electric fire would, I think, be drawn out of a cloud silently, before it could come near enough to strike....

Did he guess that he was on the verge of the most momentous discovery of the century—one which would assure his name a place among the immortals? It is fairly certain he was more interested in solving a perplexing problem than in immortality. Possibly he took it for granted that European scientists were already three steps ahead of him.

By July he had prepared a manuscript describing all his exciting experiments of the past two years, and including specific instructions for setting up a lightning rod on a tower or steeple, even to the necessary feature of a grounding wire. "Let the experiment be made," he had said. He did not make it himself, not then. For one thing, he was waiting for a spire to be erected on the top of Christ Church, from which he wished to make his first try of drawing lightning from the skies. Also, in spite of his alleged retirement, his days were becoming increasingly filled with public duties.

He still had the Gazette and *Poor Richard's Almanack* to publish and edit. Beginning in 1748, he served on the City Council.

Since 1749 he was Grand Master of the Masons. In 1751 he was made an alderman and a member of the Pennsylvania Assembly, where previously he had served as clerk.

In 1750, an American Philosophical Society member, Dr. Thomas Bond, came to him for help in starting a hospital for the sick and the insane. Hitherto those who could not pay for medical care had no choice but the prison or the almshouse. The need was urgent but Dr. Bond had failed to arouse interest in his project.

"Those whom I ask to subscribe," he confided to Franklin, "often ask me whether I have consulted you and what you think of it. When I tell them I have not, they don't subscribe."

Franklin knew promotion methods as Dr. Bond did not, and began by calling a meeting of citizens. Under his impetus the list of subscribers grew, though not until May 1755 was the cornerstone of the Pennsylvania Hospital laid on Eighth Street between Spruce and Pine. Nearly thirty years later, when Dr. Benjamin Rush joined the staff, the "lunatics" at Pennsylvania Hospital received the first intelligent care available in America and, with few exceptions, in the world.

Franklin was also busy during this period in the formation of America's first insurance company (stemming from a meeting of Philadelphia businessmen in 1752), and was taking the lead in organizing an expedition in search of a Northwest Passage, under Captain Charles Swaine, America's first voyage of Arctic exploration.

In the category of pleasure were the infrequent periods he spent on his Burlington farm, where he raised corn, red clover, herd grass and oats, recording with scientific precision the effects of frost and the results obtained from different types of soil. He was one of the earliest Americans to think of agriculture as a science. He never could persuade his farmer neighbors to follow his example. They held that the ways of their forefathers were inevitably the best.

It may have been at his farm that he made his experiment on ants. Some ants had found their way into an earthen pot of molasses. He shook out all but one and hung the pot by a string to a nail in the ceiling. When the ant had dined to its satisfaction, it climbed up the string and down the wall to the floor. Half an hour later, he noted a swarm of ants retracing its course back to the pot—exactly as though their comrade had verbally informed them where to go for a good meal.

There were few mysteries of nature on which at one time or another Franklin did not direct his attention. More often than not, he wrote his speculations in long and entertaining and gracefully phrased letters to his friends, men and women alike.

If he was not impatient to learn what Peter Collinson thought of his proposed lightning rods, it was simply that he had no time for impatience. The truth was that Collinson had found his paper fascinating and had even read it to the Royal Society. As the Society members remained skeptical and unimpressed, in 1751 he arranged for it to be printed in a pamphlet—"Experiments and Observations on Electricity, Made at Philadelphia, in America." Dr. John

Fothergill, a London physician, wrote the preface. The pamphlet was translated into French the next year, creating immediate excitement.

Three French scientists, the naturalist Count Georges Louis Buffon, Thomas François d'Alibard, and another named de Lor, resolved to carry out the experiment on drawing lightning from the skies, which Franklin had outlined.

It was d'Alibard who succeeded first. At Marly, outside of Paris, he set up a pointed iron rod forty feet long, not on a church steeple as Franklin had recommended, but simply on a square plank with legs made of three wine bottles to insulate it from the ground. During a thunderstorm, on May 10, 1752, a crash of thunder was followed by a crackling sound—and sparks flew out from the rod. Here then was absolute proof that Franklin was right. Lightning and electricity were identical.

De Lor repeated the experiment in Paris eight days later. Louis XV, King of France, was so moved that he sent congratulations to the Royal Society, to be relayed to Messieurs Franklin and Peter Collinson. The first successful experiment in London was made by John Canton. Soon it was being repeated throughout Europe. The name of Benjamin Franklin was on everyone's tongue.

No news of all this had yet been brought on the slow sailing ships when, in June 1752, Franklin decided not to wait for the completion of the Christ Church spire for his experiment. He had another scheme. Why not try to draw electricity from the skies with a kite?

"Make a small cross of two light strips of cedar, the arms so long as to reach to the four corners of a large thin silk handkerchief when extended; tie the corners of the handkerchief to the extremities of the cross." Thus he later described the body of this world famous kite. Like ordinary kites, it had a tail, loop, and string. At the top of the vertical cedar strip, he fastened a sharp pointed wire about a foot long. At the end of the string he tied a silk ribbon. He fastened a small key at the juncture of silk and twine.

With this child's plaything, he and his tall full-grown son, William, took off across the fields one threatening summer day. They let the wind raise the kite into the air and they waited. Even before it began raining, Franklin observed some loose threads from the hempen string standing erect. He pressed his knuckle to the key—and an electric spark shot out. There were more sparks when the thunderstorm began. After the string was wet, the "electric fire" was "copious."

He must have grinned triumphantly at William, and perhaps said casually, "Well, Billy, we've done it."

There is no evidence that he realized his experiment might be dangerous, even deadly.

The first account of the "Electrical Kite" appeared five months later in the October 19, 1752, issue of the *Gazette*. *Poor Richard's Almanack* for 1753 contained complete instructions on how to build a lightning rod. He had already put one up on his own chimney. It had small bells which chimed when clouds containing electricity passed by. The bells rang in his house for years.

News of his triumphs abroad were now flooding in. The praise of the French king, he wrote a friend, made him feel like the girl "who was observed to grow suddenly proud, and none could guess the reason, till it came to be known that she had got on a new pair of garters." The Royal Society, making up for lost time, published an account of his kite in *Transactions*, their official paper, and in November 1753, gave him the Copley gold medal for "his curious experiments and observations on electricity." They conservatively held off making him a member of the Society until May 29, 1756. At home, Harvard, Yale, and William and Mary College in turn gave him honorary degrees of master of arts.

While these and other tributes were being heaped on him, he was launching into a new profession—that of military expert and officer.

6
A BRIEF MILITARY CAREER

In 1753, trouble was brewing once more between Great Britain and France, with the colonists caught in the middle. While English subjects in America were as yet confined to a narrow strip along the Atlantic, France held Canada and the St. Lawrence Valley to the north; New Orleans and the great Louisiana territory in the south. By right of early explorations, the French also claimed the rich Ohio Valley region and were building forts along the Ohio and Allegheny rivers. The British considered these forts an intrusion on *their* territory.

As the situation grew more tense, both British and French courted the favor of the Indians. In Pennsylvania this would have been easier had the policy of William Penn been followed; he had gone further than any other white man in establishing friendly Indian relations. Unfortunately, much of his work had been undone by his son Thomas, in the episode known as the Walking Purchase.

To make room for his immigrants, William Penn had once purchased a tract of land from the Indians to extend "as far as a man could walk in three days." In 1683, he had leisurely walked out a day and a half of this purchase, some twenty-five miles. In 1737, fifty years later, Thomas Penn decided to take up the rest of the Walking Purchase. He hired three athletes to do the walking for him. In a day and a half, they managed to cover eighty-six miles. The Indians had never forgiven this underhanded trick.

It was partially to undo this bad feeling that in September 1753 Franklin and several other commissioners were sent by Governor James Hamilton to Carlisle, some 125 miles west of Philadelphia, to meet with chiefs of the Delaware and Shawnee Indians and the Six Nations (the name given to the united Iroquois tribes).

Franklin had never been so far inland before nor had he any previous dealings with the original Americans. He was impressed with the ceremonial exchange of gifts and greetings which preceded the actual conference. These "savages" of whom he had heard such disparaging things had customs very different from those of the white man, but "savage justice," as he was to write later, had as much to recommend it as "civilized justice."

The grievances presented by the chiefs after the conference began he found reasonable. They wanted, from the white man, fewer trading posts and more honest traders. They wanted to be sold less rum, which was ruinous to the braves, and more gunpowder, which they needed for hunting. The commissioners promised to do their best and, as they had been authorized to do, offered the Indians protection from the French, in return for their loyalty. Unfortunately, neither colonies nor British were in a position to guarantee such protection.

Franklin returned from Carlisle to learn that he had been appointed deputy postmaster, with William Hunter of Williamsburg, of all the North American provinces. He had the prestige of being an officer of the Crown though the pay was nominal—only 600 pounds a year divided between him and Hunter should the service make a profit—and the work was considerable, for Hunter was ill and could give little help.

He could and did provide his family with jobs. William, his son, became postmaster of Philadelphia, Franklin's former job. William later turned this post over to a relative of Debby's who in due time was succeeded by Franklin's brother Peter. He appointed another brother, John, postmaster of Boston. At John's death his widow succeeded him, thought to be the first American woman to hold a public office.

Not only his family but all of America profited by Franklin's appointment. Horseback riders carried mail in colonial America. Delivery was slow, irregular and costly. Franklin acted as an efficiency expert. He increased mail deliveries from Philadelphia to New York from once a week to three times a week during the warmer six months of the year and he made sure his riders did the route twice a week in the winter except in the worst weather. In time he visited all the post offices of the colonies, studied their local problems, surveyed roads, ferries, and fords. He started America's first Dead Letter Office, and gave patrons other services they had never had before. By the time he had held the post eight years, not only could he and Hunter collect their full salaries but there was a surplus for the London office, the first time it had ever profited from its American branch.

Late in 1753, Governor Robert Dinwiddie of Virginia sent young Major George Washington on a journey to the French Fort Le Boeuf (now Erie, Pennsylvania) to order the French to evacuate. They chose to ignore the warning.

Franklin attended another conference with the Six Nations, held at Albany, New

York, in June 1754, attended by commissioners from seven colonies. In regard to Indian relations, the Albany conference was no more successful than the one at Carlisle. Afterward the Indians claimed they had been persuaded to deed a tract of land whose boundaries they had not grasped and that the deed was irregular since, contrary to the Six Nations' custom, it gave away land of tribes whose representatives had not signed the deed.

Thus the two meetings had the opposite effect of what had been hoped. They succeeded only in antagonizing the Indians. Many of them decided to support the French, as the lesser of the two white evils.

It is most unlikely that Franklin suspected any wrong being perpetrated on the Indians. During the Albany conference he presented to his fellow commissioners a plan which had its inspiration from Six Nations. If the Iroquois tribes could work together harmoniously, why should the American colonies, allegedly civilized, always be quarreling? Accordingly, he proposed they form a confederacy under a single president-general appointed by the Crown.

The commissioners approved wholeheartedly but that was as far as he got. When his plan was presented to the assemblies of the various colonies, it was rejected as being too dictatorial. The Crown opposed it as being too democratic. In a final effort to make his point he published in the *Gazette* America's first cartoon, a drawing of a snake chopped in eight pieces, each marked with the initials of different colonies. "Join or Die" read the caption.

But he was several years in advance of the times.

Even while the Albany conference was under way, seven hundred French soldiers and Indians forced the surrender of Fort Necessity, a small barricade fifty miles from Wills Creek, held by George Washington, now a colonel, and a scant 400 men. The nine-year French and Indian Wars were unofficially under way.

In December, six months later, General Edward Braddock landed in Virginia with two regiments of British regulars. They had come to take the French Fort Duquesne, located on the forks of the Ohio (where Pittsburgh now stands). The Pennsylvania Assembly sent Franklin to meet the general at Frederickstown and offer his services as postmaster. Franklin with his son William spent several days with Braddock. He found the general a master of European military strategy but more than a little arrogant.

"After taking Fort Duquesne," Braddock announced one night at dinner, "I will proceed to Niagara; and, having taken that, to Frontenac, if the season will allow time; and I suppose it will, for Duquesne can hardly detain me above three or four days."

In his mind, Franklin pictured the long line of Braddock's army marching along a narrow road cut through thick woods and bushes, and he was uneasy. He was sure, he told the general, that there would be scant resistance at Duquesne, if he arrived there. The danger would be Indian ambush on the way.

Braddock smiled patronizingly. "These savages may, indeed, be a formidable enemy to your raw American militia, but upon the king's regular and disciplined troops, sir, it is impossible they should make any impression."

Franklin did not press his doubts. It would have been improper for him to argue with a military man about his own profession. Braddock was only too glad to let Franklin hunt up some transport wagons for him. This he did by distributing circulars through Lancaster, York and Cumberland counties. Within two weeks Pennsylvania farmers had come through with the loan of 150 wagons and 259 horses. Of the 1,000 pounds due the owners in payment, Braddock paid 800 and Franklin advanced the extra 200 pounds on his own. Since the farmers knew and trusted him, he, rather than Braddock, gave them his bond for the full cost.

After he returned to Philadelphia, he persuaded the Assembly to donate twenty parcels for the regiment officers, each containing six pounds of sugar, a pound of tea, six pounds of coffee, six pounds of chocolate, as well as biscuit, cheese, butter, wine, cured hams. He sent along other supplies for the soldiers, advancing 1,000 pounds more of his own money to cover the costs. Barely had he been reimbursed for his expenses thus far, when the disastrous news broke.

Braddock's army—some 1,400 British regulars and 700 colonial militiamen—was ambushed by a force of French, Canadians, and Indians on July 9, 1755, when they were within seven miles of Fort Duquesne. Terrified at the shooting from this invisible enemy, the regulars panicked. Nearly a thousand were killed or wounded, including most of the officers. George Washington, who was serving as Braddock's aide, stayed to fight a valiant rear guard action. Braddock was mortally wounded, dying four days later.

At the start of the fray, the drivers took one horse from each team and raced off, leaving wagons, food parcels and provisions to the attackers. Since Franklin had given bond, the wagon owners soon appeared, demanding recompense for their losses—a total of some 20,000 pounds. He faced ruin until October when the new British commander-in-chief, Governor Shirley, authorized government payment of the debt.

In the midst of that summer's harassment and disaster, there was one pleasant interlude. On a trip to visit Rhode Island post offices, Franklin met a delightful young lady named Catherine Ray. Middle-aged and tending to stoutness as he was, she lavished affection on him, not as a suitor but as someone to whom she could confide her innermost thoughts. Though he saw Catherine only infrequently after that meeting, she later married a worthy young man named William Greene by whom she had six children—she and Franklin wrote each other lengthy and intimate letters as long as they lived. Until he met her, apart from Debby, his friendships had all been with men. Beginning with Catherine, he had many women friends, who found in him a rare understanding of their qualities of mind and spirit.

The defeat of Braddock taught the colonists that the British military was not as invincible as they had been led to believe. Many more Indians joined the French, deciding they were most likely to win. In the summer of 1755, Indian raiders were attacking isolated farms less than 100 miles from Philadelphia. It was obvious that once again Pennsylvania must provide its own defense.

A bill to vote 60,000 pounds for the militia was presented to the Pennsylvania Assembly. At first the Quakers opposed it, but with great tact Franklin won from them a concession that even though they bore no arms themselves they would not object if others did so. There was still more dissension on the subject of taxes. Franklin and many others believed that the taxes should be raised from all the landholders in the province. The lawyer for "the proprietors" claimed that the Penn family should be exempt from such taxes, as they always had been. He was supported by the conservatives in the Assembly and by Governor Robert Hunter Morris, who owed his appointment to the Penns.

Eventually the Penns compromised by offering 5,000 pounds toward the militia as a gift. The question as to whether or not their vast lands should be taxed remained unsettled, to trouble the future.

Thomas Penn, who was living in London, was duly informed that Benjamin Franklin was a crafty man who could bend the Assembly to his will.

On November 24, 1755, a Shawnee war party burned down the Moravian village of Gnadenhuetten, 75 miles from Philadelphia, killing all the inhabitants except a few who escaped into the forests. The crime was the more appalling since the Moravians were as opposed to violence as the Quakers. They were a gentle, devout people who had befriended the Indians. The next day the Assembly appointed Franklin to head a committee of seven to manage the funds for the defense. More responsibilities on his shoulders, more decisions to make, arguments to settle, hotheads to calm down.

"All the world claims the privilege of troubling my Pappy," wailed Deborah to a clerk named Daniel Fisher whom Franklin had just hired.

A few weeks later Franklin set out on horseback with 50 cavalrymen to recruit volunteers, and check on defenses in outlying districts—a strenuous assignment for a man nearly fifty and sedentary in his habits. William served as his aide. Theoretically, James Hamilton, a former governor, was in charge, but after a few days he quietly yielded the leadership to Franklin.

Their first stop was Bethlehem, the chief Moravian settlement. Franklin had expected them to be as opposed to military defense as the Quakers. On the contrary, they were determined to avoid a tragedy such as that at Gnadenhuetten, had built a stockade around their principal buildings, brought in arms from New York, and were even arming their women with small paving stones to throw out the windows should any marauding Indians approach.

"General Franklin," the Moravians insisted on calling the head of the Philadelphia expedition.

They rode on to Easton next, to find a town in a state of panic and disorder with no discipline at all. Refugees filled the houses. Food was almost gone. There was drinking and rioting. Franklin organized a guard, put sentries on the principal street, set up a patrol, had bushes outside of town cleared away to avert their use as ambush, and enlisted some two hundred men into the provincial militia.

They visited other towns, arriving at the ruins of Gnadenhuetten in the bitter cold of January. After the mournful chore of burying the dead, the men set to building a stockade—felling pines, placing them firmly in the ground side by side.

Franklin, with his passion for collecting facts, noted that it took six men six minutes to fell a pine of 14-inch diameter, and he observed that his men were more cheerful on the days they worked than when, because of rain or snow, they had to sit idle.

Supplies were running low when provisions arrived from Philadelphia, including roast beef, veal, and apples from Deborah. To reassure her, he wrote that he was sleeping on a featherbed under warm blankets. The truth was that, like his men, he slept on the floor of a hut with only one thin blanket. The stockade, finished at last, was 450 feet in circumference, 12 feet high, and had two mounted swivel guns but no cannon.

They were aware of the danger lurking in the dense forest. On a patrol, Franklin found the remains of Indian watches. For their fires they dug holes about three feet deep. The prints in weeds and grass showed they had lain in a circle around the fire holes, letting their feet hang over to keep warm. At a short distance, neither flame, sparks, nor smoke could be seen. But the Indians, not then nor later, risked an attack.

Franklin's militia did no fighting but they turned defenseless regions into defensive ones. They had built two more stockades at Fort Norris and Fort Allen, when Franklin was called back to Philadelphia early in February for a special Assembly meeting. To have a good bed again seemed so strange, he hardly slept all night long.

On his return he was appointed a militia colonel. Following his first review of his regiment, the men accompanied him to his house and saluted him with several rounds of fire, incidentally breaking some glass tubes of his electrical apparatus. The following day when he set off for Virginia on post office business, 20 officers and some 30 grenadiers escorted him to the ferry, the grenadiers riding with drawn swords in a ceremony reserved for persons of great distinction. When Thomas Penn in England learned of this tribute, he was furious. No grenadiers had ever drawn their swords for him.

As for Governor Morris, he suavely suggested that Franklin and his command should try to take Fort Duquesne, which Braddock had failed to take, promising him a general's commission. Franklin firmly declined. He had no illusions about his military ability and likely suspected Morris of wishing to be rid of him. (Fort Duquesne was eventually captured in 1758, in an expedition led by British Brigadier General Forbes; George

Washington hoisted the British flag over the fort's ruins.)

In August 1756, following a declaration of war on the Delaware, the new governor, William Denny, offered large bounties for "the scalp of every male Indian enemy above the age of twelve years," and smaller bounties for "female Indian prisoners and youths under eight." Franklin, like the majority of the Assembly members, was outraged at this barbarity, and disgusted with the conduct of the proprietors and their representatives. Early in 1757, a vote was passed to send Franklin to England, as official agent of Pennsylvania, there to present to Parliament and the King a petition of grievances against the Penns.

Debby would not go with him. She was frightened to death of the sea. He did take William, who was radiant at seeing England. By April they were in New York, ready to catch their ship. Packets for England were in charge of Lord Loudon, the new commander-in-chief, an amiable person with all the time in the world to listen to complaints, indulge in long conversations, and to write endless notes. Not until he had finished this mysterious correspondence, would he permit the fleet to depart. For more than two months, Franklin and his son waited, restless and impatient and helpless.

There was plenty of time to puzzle about the errors of the British. Why they should send to the colonies an arrogant man like General Braddock, a dawdler like Loudon, governors like the dishonest Sir William Keith, or Morris and Denny, who were far more interested in protecting the rich proprietors than in the welfare of the colonists. But then the reason for Franklin's voyage was to correct such mistakes. He had no doubt that the King and the mighty Parliament would be glad to listen to him.

7
THE BATTLE WITH THE PENNS

During the voyage to England, Franklin wrote a preface for his 1758 *Almanack*. In the form of a letter from "Poor Richard" to his "Courteous Reader," it told of a sermon on frugality and industry, which Poor Richard had heard in the market place by "a plain clean old man with white locks" called Father Abraham. He was most flattered to find that Father Abraham was quoting him, Poor Richard, at every other breath.

As Poor Richard says: Many words won't fill a bushel.... God helps them that help themselves.... The sleeping fox catches no poultry.... Early to bed, early to rise, makes a man healthy, wealthy, and wise.... For want of a nail the shoe was lost; for want of a shoe the horse was lost; and for want of a horse the rider was lost....

As Poor Richard says: Many a little makes a mickle.... Fools make feasts, and wise men eat them.... Pride that dines on vanity, sups on contempt.... 'Tis hard for an empty bag to stand upright.... If you will not hear reason, she'll surely rap your knuckles...

All the nuggets of wise counsel which he had dropped in his *Almanack* in the twenty-five years of its existence, Franklin gathered for Father Abraham's speech. Omitted were the racy ballads, verses, broad humor and jokes which had made the *Almanack* a potpourri where every man could find something to his taste. Only at the end was a touch of Franklin's sly wit. Following Father

Abraham's sermon, Poor Richard watched disconsolately as the village folk dispersed to spend their hard-earned money as foolishly as ever on the marketplace wares. The only one to take the sermon to heart was Poor Richard himself who had come to buy material for a new coat but left, "resolved to wear my old one a little longer."

Father Abraham's speech was later published under the title of "The Way to Wealth." It was reprinted in many editions and translated in many languages, and it won the author almost as much fame as his discoveries in electricity.

Peter Collinson met Franklin and his son in London, where they arrived on July 26, 1757, taking them to his home. No doubt he and Franklin discussed electricity until very late, with William only half listening and more or less bored. The next day, a printer named William Strahan, with whom Franklin had corresponded some fourteen years but never met, called on him.

"I never saw a man who was, in every respect, so perfectly agreeable to me," Strahan wrote Deborah Franklin of this meeting, adding that William was "one of the prettiest young gentlemen I ever knew from America."

Deborah likely scowled. It was just like that artful lad to ingratiate himself so quickly.

A few days later father and son rented four rooms from a widow, Mrs. Margaret Stevenson, who lived with her young daughter Polly in a substantial mansion on 7 Craven Street, Strand. This was to be Franklin's English home, which over the years became almost as dear to him as his Philadelphia one.

He had brought two servants with him. One of them, Peter, served him faithfully, though the other, a slave, ran away shortly after their arrival. Franklin's post as Massachusetts agent required a bit of pomp. He wore a wig in the latest fashion, silver shoe and knee buckles and purchased linen for new shirts. Later he rented a coach.

Barely was he settled when he was invited to visit Lord George Grenville, president of the Privy Council and one of England's most important statesmen. This was Franklin's first test in holding his own with persons more steeped than he in political intrigue.

Lord Grenville received him with great civility, questioned him at length about American affairs, and then announced that the colonists had some erroneous notions he felt duty bound to correct:

"You Americans have wrong ideas of the nature of your constitution; you contend that the King's instructions to his governors are not laws, and think yourselves at liberty to regard or disregard them at your own discretion. You must be made to understand that the King's instruction are *The Law of the Land.*"

This was simply not true. The King's instructions were laws in the colonies only if they received the approval of the local Assembly. In the same way, laws passed by a colonial Assembly had to be submitted to the King before they became final. That was why Franklin was in England, to get the King's approval of the Assembly decision on the Penns.

Sure as he was of his facts, he voiced his opinion in the manner he had learned from Socrates: "It is my understanding that ..."

"You are totally mistaken," Lord Grenville stated patronizingly, when he had finished.

It was Franklin's first experience with the contemptuous attitude which certain of the British took in regard to the colonists. He would later observe that "every man in England seems to jostle himself into the throne with the King, and talks of *our subjects* in the colonies."

Around the middle of August he called on the Penn family, at their stately mansion in Spring Garden. It had seemed courteous to meet with them personally before approaching higher authority. William Penn's son Thomas was there and probably Richard Penn and his son, John. They received him with glacial politeness, listened haughtily as he told them the Assembly's grievances, and just as haughtily denied that the grievances were in any way justified.

Franklin pointed out that the Assembly was asking no more than what William Penn had promised citizens under his 1701 Charter of Privileges.

"My father granted privileges he had no right to grant, according to the Royal Charter," Thomas Penn announced.

"Then all those who came to settle in the province, expecting to enjoy the privileges contained in the grant were deceived, cheated and betrayed?" With the greatest difficulty, Franklin kept his voice calm.

Thomas Penn laughed insolently. "If the people were cheated, it was their own fault. They should have gone to the trouble of reading the Royal Charter."

His tone reminded Franklin of a horse trader of low character, jeering at the purchaser he had victimized. "Poor people are not lawyers," he said steadily. "They trusted your father and did not think it necessary to consult a lawyer."

Unabashed, Thomas Penn rose to dismiss him. "If you care to put your complaints in writing, Mr. Franklin, we will then consider them."

Those arrogant Penns! How it would have grieved their noble father to see into what selfish hands he had left his beloved Pennsylvania! Franklin had yet to find out through personal experience that nobility of character is not always inherited.

Five days later he returned with the Assembly's grievances in written form. On the advice of their lawyer, a "proud and angry man," Ferdinand John Paris, the Penns sent Franklin's paper to the Royal lawyers, the Attorney-General Charles Pratt, and Solicitor-General Charles Yorke. These gentlemen were out of town. There was nothing to do but wait.

Franklin fell sick with a cold and fever that September and was bedridden nearly eight weeks. Dr. Fothergill, the man who had written the preface for his pamphlet on electricity, tended him regularly. Mrs. Stevenson, his landlady, nursed him like a son. Even William was unusually obliging, did his errands and helped him to prepare a letter to the *Citizen* to counteract slanders about Pennsylvania which Franklin suspected emanated from the Penns. William was enrolling in law school in London; he had bought himself elegant clothes that rivaled those of any young English peer.

As soon as he was well enough, Franklin went on a shopping spree himself. For Debby, who still liked bright colors, he purchased a crimson satin cloak and for Sally a black silk one, with a scarlet feather and muff which William selected. There were other luxuries for their home not found in America: English china, silver salt ladles, an apple corer and a gadget "to make little turnips out of great ones," a carpet, tablecloths, napkins, silk blankets from France, and a "large fine jug for beer," which he had fallen in love with at first sight.

"I thought it looked like a fat jolly dame," he explained the gift to Debby, "clean and tidy, with a neat blue and white calico gown on, good-natured and lovely, and put me in mind of—somebody."

His most extravagant present followed later—a harpsichord for Sally which cost the huge sum of forty-two guineas.

If some Englishmen were snobs, there were plenty of others who were just the opposite. Franklin's fellow members of the august Royal Society welcomed him warmly. He made many new scientific friends, among them the stout and amiable John Pringle, an authority on military medicine and sanitation, and John Canton, the first Englishman to draw lightning from the sky. At Cambridge, in May 1758, he performed experiments in evaporation with John Hadley, professor of chemistry. He made a trip to Northampton, the ancestral home of the Franklins, and met some distant relatives. When he found the Franklin graves in the cemetery so moss covered that their inscriptions were effaced, he had his servant Peter scour them clean.

The Scottish University of St. Andrews gave him a degree as doctor of law.

Henceforth he had the right to call himself Dr. Franklin. Later he visited Scotland where he was made an honorary burgess and guildbrother at Edinburgh; met the economist Adam Smith; and the philosopher David Hume, who said of him: "America has sent us many good things, gold, silver, sugar, tobacco, indigo, etc., but you are the first philosopher, and indeed the first great man of letters, for whom we are beholden to her."

He stayed with the congenial Scottish judge Lord Henry Home Kames, to whom he wrote in his note of thanks that the time spent in Scotland "was six weeks of the *densest* happiness I have met with in any part of my life."

A bitter fellow American arrived in London, William Smith, provost of the Pennsylvania Academy, one of those who had opposed him on the Penn issue. The Pennsylvania Assembly had tried him on the charge of libel and he had spent three months in jail. Now he was seeking redress from the Crown, and blaming not only the Quakers for his arrest but Franklin, who had not even been in Pennsylvania. Smith was saying that Franklin was not really a scientist, that he had stolen his ideas from others.

Franklin took the slander philosophically: "'Tis convenient to have at least one enemy, who by his readiness to revile one on all occasions may make one careful of one's conduct. I shall keep him an enemy for that purpose."

While the proprietors were stalling, Franklin set out to meet such high-placed persons as might help his cause. He tried to see the Prime Minister William Pitt, who was said to be sympathetic to the colonies, but Pitt was too occupied with his enormous war in India to give him a hearing. Eventually he met the two royal lawyers, Charles Yorke and Charles Pratt, to whom the Penns had submitted the Assembly's grievances. To his surprise he found they had already given their verdict, a negative one, which the Penns had forwarded directly to the Assembly, bypassing Franklin. The Penns were claiming he had insulted them. He had not addressed them as the "True and Absolute Proprietaries of the Province of Pennsylvania."

Back in Pennsylvania, the Assembly had finally persuaded Governor Denny to pass its act taxing the proprietary estate. Franklin brought the matter before the British Committee for Plantation Affairs in August 1759, when he had been two years in England. The decision was a compromise: unsurveyed lands of the proprietors should not be taxed but their surveyed lands must be taxed at a rate no higher than other similar lands. The

Pennsylvania Assembly held Franklin solely responsible for the victory, and congratulations flowed to him.

He could have gone home now but he stayed on. There was a tremendous propaganda job to be done and he was the only one capable. He wanted to set the English straight on the role of the American colonies in the British Empire. He wrote articles for the press. He expressed his ideas at the Whig Club, in coffeehouses where philosophers and literary men congregated, and to guests whom he invited to dine at Craven Street. His refreshing candor and quiet wit brought him attention everywhere.

At odd moments he tinkered with various inventions. For the Stevensons, he devised an iron frame with a sliding plate to serve as a draught in their fireplace, so it would give more heat and take less fuel.

He made a clock with only three wheels and one hand, which showed hours, minutes, and seconds. Later others improved his model and sold it commercially.

He spent long hours constructing a musical instrument, based on the principle of musical glasses. The "armonica" he named it, remarking that it was "peculiarly adapted to Italian music, especially that of the soft and plaintive kind." Subsequently, an English musician, Marianne Davies, toured the Continent giving armonica recitals; Marie Antoinette took lessons from her. Mozart and Beethoven composed selections for the armonica. Its vogue lasted some fifty years, and then, no one knows just why, it lost its popularity.

In August 1761, he took William on a trip to Belgium and Holland. In Brussels, the Prince of Lorraine welcomed him and showed him his physics laboratory. At Leyden, he met Musschenbroek, inventor of the Leyden jar. They were back in time for the coronation of George III, whom Franklin judged "a virtuous and generous young man."

In February 1762, Oxford University gave the honorary degree of doctor of civil laws to "the illustrious Benjamin Franklin, Esquire, Agent of the Province of Pennsylvania, Postmaster-General of North America, and Fellow of the Royal Society." Less ostentatiously, William was presented a degree of master of arts.

William had been basking in the sunlight of his father's reputation, and Franklin had more than a little reason to worry about him. Unlike his father, the youth was proud and haughty and disdainful of those of humble birth.

One day Franklin told him a story. When he was a child of seven, Franklin said, some friends on a holiday filled his pocket with coppers. He went directly to a toy shop, and being charmed with the sound of a whistle in the hands of another boy, he gave all his money for one like it. He came home and went whistling all over the house, much pleased with his purchase, until his brothers, sisters, and cousins told him he had given four times as much as it was worth, laughing at him for his folly. Put in mind of the good things he might have bought with the rest of the money, he cried with vexation. "The reflection gave me more chagrin than the whistle gave me pleasure."

"As I grew older," he continued, "I have found a number of men who have given too much for their whistle—popularity-seekers, misers, and men of pleasure. Don't give too much for the whistle, William. Why not become a joiner or wheelwright, if the estate I leave you is not enough? The man who lives by his labor is at least free."

Did little Benjamin really spend all his pennies for a whistle, or was this a fable which Franklin invented to clothe a moral lesson? There is no way of knowing for sure and it is not important. It should be emphasized that the story, or fable, was not intended merely to show the folly of wasting money. It had a far more subtle meaning.

Much as Franklin had come to love England, his heart was heavy with yearning for his family and his own country after his five year absence. Since England and France were still at war, he had to wait for a safe convoy. It was August 1762 when he set sail from Portsmouth. William did not come with him. The Crown had appointed him to the high post of governor of New Jersey. He would take a later ship, after his papers were in order.

"Don't give too much for the whistle," Franklin may have warned him once more before he left.

8
THE WHITE CHRISTIAN SAVAGES

"Benjamin Franklin has lost all his Philadelphia friends."

That was the rumor which his "enemy," William Smith, had been spreading. It had reached Franklin's ears but he had not worried about it nor did he have reason to. As his ship sailed into port, in November 1762, the docks were bright with waving flags and packed with cheering crowds. Five hundred horsemen escorted him home.

Waiting for him were Debby, his "plain country Joan," stout, beaming, and vociferous in her greeting, and his daughter Sally, pretty and elegant in the London frocks he had sent her. From morning to night in the next days, his Philadelphia friends, those whom Smith said he did not have, were filling his house, boisterous and hearty, slapping him on the back, congratulating him on the job he had done, in every way possible showing him their warm and lasting affection.

Did he find their manners a bit rough, their horizon of knowledge limited after his cultured and learned English friends? Nostalgically he wrote to Polly Stevenson: "Why should that little island (England) enjoy in almost every neighbourhood more sensible, virtuous, and elegant minds than we can collect in ranging a hundred leagues of our vast forests?"

Not that America would always remain behind England in the arts: "Already some of our young geniuses begin to lisp attempts at painting poetry and music." And with his letter he proudly included some American verse he thought might find favor in England.

The supporters of the proprietors were still criticizing him, claiming now that Benjamin Franklin had lived extravagantly and wasted public money in England. They were disappointed rather than gratified when he submitted to the Assembly a bill for his five years' expenses—for just 714 pounds, ten shillings, seven pence. The Assembly, too embarrassed to accept such a modest estimate, promptly voted him 3,000 pounds.

In February, William arrived to take up his office as New Jersey's royal governor, bringing with him a beautiful and dignified new bride, Elizabeth, who had been born in the West Indies. Franklin toured New Jersey with them, along with an escort of cavalry and gentlemen on sleighs. His heart filled with pride as he saw the respect and affection with which they were welcomed by rich and poor alike, and his fears about William were for the moment put aside.

He did some 1,600 miles traveling of his own from the Spring to the fall of 1763, the first year of his return, taking up where he had left off in expanding and improving the colonial postal services. Sally went with him on one trip up to New England, when they stayed with the former Catherine Ray, now Mrs. William Greene, her husband a future governor of Rhode Island. When he dislocated his shoulder in a fall from his horse, it was Catherine who nursed him. The friendships of Benjamin Franklin—how much could be said of them! He guarded them all, men and women alike, more preciously than jewels, nourished them with letters during separations, and with personal warmth during reunions.

In February 1763, the Treaty of Paris brought the French and Indian Wars to a formal close in England's favor, but did not solve the tensions between colonists and Indians which the struggle had fomented.

Though the treaty granted the Indians the lands from the Allegheny Mountains to the Mississippi, the Indians had learned to be suspicious of the white man's treaties and rightly feared that future settlers would drive them back further and further. Out of desperation, they attacked English garrisons from Detroit to Fort Pitt.

The English reciprocated ruthlessly. One British general suggested that blankets inoculated with smallpox be presented to them "to extirpate this execrable race." As contagious as any disease was the racial hatred that spread along the frontiers. In Lancaster County, certain Scotch-Irish settlers of Paxton and Donegal townships met together and vowed vengeance on the "redskins." "The only good Indian is a dead Indian," they said. If the warring Indians vanished into the forests after each assault, why then there were plenty of others—such as those living under the protection of the good Moravians.

In December, the Paxton Boys, as they called themselves, attacked a tiny hamlet of peaceful Conestoga Indians. Six were killed outright. Fourteen others, old people, women and children, who had been out selling baskets, brooms and bowls to their white neighbors, were taken captive and lodged at the Lancaster workhouse. Two days after Christmas, the rioters broke into the workhouse, killing all of them with hatchets. Streams of other peaceful Indians poured into Philadelphia for protection.

William Penn's grandson, John Penn, was now Pennsylvania's governor. He ordered the arrest of the murderers but did nothing to enforce his order. Made bold by this seeming lack of concern, the Paxton Boys, their ranks swollen by a lawless mob, voted to go to Philadelphia and force the Assembly to turn over the Indian refugees to their untender mercies.

Franklin's war activities had shown he condemned atrocities against the frontiersmen, but he was outraged that Indians who had kept faith with the white men should have been betrayed. By mid-January he had both written and printed a pamphlet, "Narrative of the Late Massacres in Lancaster County."

The first part retold the story of Indian relations in Pennsylvania. How members of the Six Nations had first settled in Conestoga, how its messengers had welcomed the English with presents of venison, corn and skins, how the tribe had entered into a treaty of friendship with William Penn, to last "as long as the sun should shine or the waters run in the rivers."

It was an "enormous wickedness," he continued, to assassinate these Conestoga Indians for the sins of the "rum-debauched, trader-corrupted vagabonds and thieves on the Susquehanna and Ohio." It was as illogical as if the Dutch should seek revenge on the English for injuries done by the French, merely because both English and French were white.

To what good, he asked, had Old Shehaes, so ancient he had been present at Penn's Treaty in 1701, been cut to pieces in his bed? What was to be gained by shooting or killing with a hatchet little boys and girls—and a one-year-old baby? "This is done by no civilized nation in Europe. Do we come to America to learn and practise the manners of barbarians?" The Conestoga Indians would have been safe among the ancient heathen, the Turks, the Saracens, the Moors, the Spanish, the Negroes—anywhere in the world "except in the neighborhood of the Christian white savages."

Christian white savages! That was a phrase to make people wince. Those who shared the prejudices of the Paxton Boys were highly indignant. But the Quakers agreed with him, and the pamphlet convinced a surprising number of others that it was their duty to defend their city and protect the Indians who had sought refuge with them.

Panic spread as the Paxton rioters, armed and in an ugly mood, approached Philadelphia. In the emergency Governor John Penn turned to Franklin to reorganize his militia. Almost overnight a thousand citizens rallied to arms, among them Junto members and firemen. On February 8, word came that the mob was at the city limits. The governor, with his councilors, rushed to Franklin at midnight, seeking advice. His house became their temporary headquarters.

The ford over the Schuylkill River was guarded. The Paxton group bypassed it, turned north, crossed the river at another ford, and came noisily into Germantown some ten miles from Philadelphia.

"You go talk to them, Franklin," pleaded the frightened governor.

Benjamin rode off to Germantown with only three of his men, and spoke with the mob's leaders so reasonably and sternly they agreed to turn back. Three days later they had all gone home and quiet was restored to the city.

"For about 48 hours, I was a very great man," he wrote Lord Kames. To Dr. Fothergill in London, he tersely described his activities: "Your old friend was a common soldier, a councillor, a kind of dictator, an ambassador to a country mob, and, on his returning home, nobody again."

The help he had given in a delicate situation did not win him the governor's approval. To his Uncle Thomas Penn he wrote on May 5 that there would never be "any prospect of ease and happiness while that villain has the liberty of spreading about the poison of that inveterate malice and ill nature which is deeply implanted in his own black heart."

Instead of bringing the Paxton criminals to justice, John Penn launched a bitter attack on the Pennsylvania Assembly, whom he called "arrogant usurpers." The Assembly membership promptly voted as president their most controversial member, Benjamin Franklin.

The annual elections for Assembly seats were held in October 1764. Two parties sprang up: Old Ticket, which supported Franklin and Joseph Galloway, another liberal, as candidates; New Ticket, the conservatives, the supporters of the Penns, and the Indian haters in whose hearts still rankled Franklin's phrase, "white Christian savages." The campaign was stormy and there was mud slinging on both sides. In Philadelphia, Old Ticket lost by 25 votes out of 4,000. Galloway was upset. Franklin merely shrugged and went home to bed.

Only in Philadelphia had the New Ticket won. When the returns came in from the rest of the province, Old Ticket still had a majority in the Assembly. They convened on October 26, and voted to send the King a petition begging him to take back the province from the Penns, making it a royal province. Franklin prepared the petition and was selected to take it in person to England. John Penn was blind with fury but helpless.

Franklin was engaged in having a new house built on Market Street between Third and Fourth. It was of brick, thirty-four feet square, with three rooms to each floor, and it had a pleasant garden. The kitchen was in the cellar with a special arrangement of pipes "to carry off steam and smell and smoke." It would naturally be protected by a lightning rod and would be heated by the now celebrated Franklin stoves.

He did not like to leave his house unfinished and he dreaded another separation from Debby, who was still terrified at the thought of an Atlantic crossing. But the long political squabble had bored and wearied him, and he looked forward to seeing England and his English friends again.

"I will be gone only a few months," he assured his wife and his pretty daughter, when he left them in November 1764. He could not then guess that the few months would stretch to more than ten years.

9
THE STAMP ACT

His ship, the *King of Prussia*, reached Portsmouth in just thirty days. By December 11, 1764, he was ensconced once more at 7 Craven Street, in the tender care of Polly and Mrs. Stevenson, exuberant to have their kind American friend with them once more. How pleasant to be spoiled by them, to resume his dinners at the Royal Society, his meetings with his scientific colleagues, to see again his many English acquaintances!

In respect to his mission, his return was less satisfactory. The Penn family was as influential as ever. For nearly two years, their scheming prevented him from getting the Assembly petition so much as a hearing by the King's Privy Council. When at last, in November 1766, the hearing was granted, the answer was short and decisive: the King had no power to interfere with the rights of the proprietors of a province. The petition was denied.

Franklin tried in vain to have the decision reversed. The proprietors officially retained their claims on Pennsylvania for ten years more, until the events of 1776 changed the whole structure of the American provinces.

An even more urgent crisis retained him in London. Lord George Grenville, the same who had so blatantly stated that the King's word was law in the colonies, was now chief adviser to George III. His situation was precarious and he knew that his cabinet was doomed if he failed to raise some money. And where would one find money if not by taxing the American colonies? Since the Americans had no representation in Parliament, no votes would be lost even should the colonists grumble at being taxed.

So Grenville reasoned, and it was thus that he conceived foisting the Stamp Act on the colonies. The Act was to tax some fifty-five articles, including all legal papers, advertisements, and marriage licenses. A liquor license required a tax of four pounds; a pack of cards, one shilling; a pair of dice, ten shillings. A newspaper on a half-sheet of paper must carry a stamp worth one half-penny. A civil appointment worth more than twenty pounds a year took a four-pound tax. A college degree cost two pounds in taxes.

Grenville called the colonial agents together and discussed his brainstorm with them. The money raised, he assured them, would be used in America—for public works and for the maintenance of British troops to protect them. If they had any better idea for levying taxes, they should tell him. The agents, Franklin among them, could only point out that no taxes would be popular; that if Parliament needed money, the proper procedure was to ask the Assemblies to raise what they could.

Their objections were ignored. Politically, America was then in disfavor. The English held that the seven-year struggle with France, with its huge expenditure in lives and money, had saved the thirteen colonies from French tyranny. They should be grateful. They should want to help reduce the national debt. Instead they were always clamoring for something or other.

In quick succession the Stamp Act passed the House of Lords and the House of

Commons, and was approved by the King on March 22, 1765, scheduled to go into effect on November 1. Franklin felt that a bad mistake had been made, but that, since the Stamp Act was now a law, it should be obeyed until a way was found to get it repealed. To an American friend he wrote that he opposed it "sincerely and heartily." He added philosophically, "Idleness and pride tax with a heavier hand than kings and parliaments; if we can get rid of the former, we may easily bear the latter."

Grenville summoned Franklin to a conference. Was it not a good idea to appoint Americans as stamp officers to distribute the stamps, so that the colonists could deal with their own? Did Franklin have anyone to suggest? Franklin proposed two—John Hughes of Pennsylvania, who needed a job, and Jared Ingersoll, agent for Connecticut. Somehow it did not occur to him that he was throwing himself open to criticism at home.

An attack of gout kept him in bed for some time after the passage of the Act. He amused himself with one of his hoaxes, a letter to the newspapers mocking certain alleged economists who claimed that the colonies could never be self-supporting.

In America, he wrote, the "very tails of the American sheep are so laden with wool, that each has a little car or wagon on four little wheels, to support and keep it from trailing on the ground." Wool was so cheap and plentiful that colonists spread it on the floors of the horses' stalls instead of straw.

He next described a mythical "cod and whale fishery" on the Great Lakes. Did people imagine that cod and whale lived only in salt water? They should know how cod fled from whales into any safe water, salt or fresh, and how the whales pursued them: "The grand leap of the whale in the chase up the falls of Niagara is esteemed, by all who have seen it, as one of the finest spectacles in nature."

Soon all London was chuckling about the whale that leaped up the Niagara.

In the meantime a tempest was erupting in America. The Stamp Act which Franklin had taken so calmly had evoked a clamor throughout the colonies, loudest in New England and Virginia. At the House of Burgesses in lovely Williamsburg, an eloquent young Virginian named Patrick Henry rose to declare the act "illegal, unconstitutional, and unjust," and to spout a set of resolutions, defining the rights of colonists as British subjects, as had never been done so effectively. The Virginia Resolves were printed in all the colonial newspapers, setting aflame a smoldering indignation. A new organization, the Sons of Liberty, held parades and protest meetings.

Franklin was plainly shocked. "The rashness of the Assembly in Virginia is amazing," he wrote John Hughes, his appointee as stamp officer. "A firm loyalty to the Crown ... will always be the wisest course." The stupid Lord Grenville had been succeeded in July by the Marquis of Rockingham. Franklin was hopeful he could be persuaded of the folly and injustice of the tax. All that was needed was patience.

But the word patience had no appeal in America. When the names of the stamp officers were published in August, riots broke out from New Hampshire to South Carolina. Mobs gathered in front of the house of John Hughes, burning him in effigy, threatening him with hanging and drowning, until he was forced to resign. Similar demonstrations forced resignations from Jared Ingersoll and other stamp officers. By the time the stamps arrived, there were almost no officers to distribute them. As a further measure, the colonists began to boycott British goods, to the sorrow of the British merchants who henceforth became the most ardent advocates of repeal.

The Penn supporters took advantage of the fray to point out that it was Lord Grenville who was responsible for the hated act—not the proprietors. As for Benjamin Franklin, everyone in England knew he was on excellent terms with Grenville. In the stormy atmosphere, exaggeration mounted to falsehood. Soon people were saying that Franklin had framed the act, helped to get it passed, and accepted pay for recommending the stamp officers.

Debby became marked as the wife of the man who had betrayed his trust, and old friends slighted her on the street. There were rumblings about burning their handsome new home. Governor William Franklin worriedly came to try to persuade her and Sally to take refuge with him in New Jersey. She let Sally go but refused to budge herself.

Cool-headedly and courageously, she collected guns and ammunition and enough provisions to see her through a siege. Her brother came to stay with her as did one of Franklin's nephews. The house was turned into an arsenal. But no attacks were made. In her heart Debby was sure there would be none. Why should anyone want to hurt her or Pappy?

The object of this fury was in that very period working tirelessly to achieve repeal by peaceful means. "I was extremely busy," he wrote Lord Kames, "attending members of both Houses, informing, explaining, consulting, disputing, in a continual hurry from morning to night."

He conferred with leading statesmen, such as Lord Dartmouth, so much respected in America that a college was named for him. He dined with the Minister Lord Rockingham, and found an ally in Rockingham's private secretary, a gifted Irishman named Edmund Burke. He sought out the manufacturers and merchants who were suffering from the American boycott, and enlisted their support. He wrote letters to newspapers to convince England's common people that the Stamp Act was a major obstacle to Anglo-American friendship.

He used his charm, his wit, his power of persuasion, his writing talents, his high reputation as a scientist, all as weapons to win friends for the American cause. The other colonial agents worked with him, but none could equal his activities. The news from America saddened him and he knew he had to fight, not only to save his own prestige, but to preserve what then seemed to him terribly important—the harmony between the colonists and the Crown.

Finally, in February 1766, there was a breakthrough in the wall of seeming indifference. The House of Commons summoned him to answer questions of the probable effects of the Stamp Act in America. He was dead with fatigue and troubled with gout, but inwardly he was jubilant. He had coached his friends in Parliament in advance on what to ask, and guessed without difficulty the line of inquiry of the opposition.

"What is your name and place of abode?" the Speaker asked first.

"Franklin of Philadelphia," he said, as if there were no need to be more explicit.

For three hours the questions rained down on him. He answered fully, drawing from his vast knowledge of American affairs. As he spoke in his dry quiet voice, peering at the House members over his spectacles, he gave the impression of a schoolmaster instructing a group of students.

"Do the Americans pay any considerable taxes among themselves?" asked James Hewitt, Member for Coventry, a town that manufactured the worsteds and ribbons which the colonists had stopped buying.

They paid many and heavy taxes, Franklin said. He enumerated them precisely, stressing the debt contracted in the recent war, stressing too that people of the frontier counties were so impoverished by enemy raids they could contribute nothing.

"From the thinness of the back settlements, would not the Stamp Act be extremely inconvenient to the inhabitants?" This was certainly a question he had formulated himself.

It definitely would, Franklin said. "Many of the inhabitants could not get stamps when they had occasion for them without taking long journeys and spending perhaps three or four pounds that the Crown might get sixpence."

There were many more questions and then the Stamp Act's creator, Lord Grenville, asked sharply, "Do you think it right that America should be protected by this country and pay no part of the expense?"

"That is not the case," Franklin told them. "The colonies raised, clothed, and paid, during the last war, near 25,000 men and spent many millions." Though they were supposed to be reimbursed by Parliament, in actual fact they received only a small part of their expenses. "Pennsylvania, in particular, disbursed about 500,000 pounds and the reimbursements in the whole did not exceed 60,000 pounds."

He had at his fingertips equally factual data on every subject that arose.

Someone asked, "Do you not think the people of America would submit to pay the stamp duty if it was moderated?"

"No, never," Franklin stated, "unless compelled by force of arms."

Another asked, "What was the temper of America toward Great Britain before the year 1763?"

He replied, "The best in the world. They submitted willingly to the government of the Crown, and paid, in all their courts, obedience to the acts of Parliament.... They had not only a respect but an affection for Great Britain."

"And what is their temper now?" he was asked.

"Oh, very much altered," he assured them.

"What used to be the pride of the Americans?"

"To indulge in the fashions and manufactures of Great Britain."

"What is now their pride?"

"To wear their old clothes over again till they can make new ones," he said calmly.

The session ended with this verbal blow leaving them gasping.

He had never considered himself a public speaker, and never before or after spoken so long before such a large audience, but he had won his point. In less than a month, on March 8, the Stamp Act repeal had passed both houses of Parliament and received the reluctant assent of the King. Franklin's "Examination" was published in London, and later that year in Boston, New York, Philadelphia, Williamsburg, and elsewhere in the colonies. It was translated into French and German.

It was a wonderful victory. There was rejoicing throughout America. Philadelphia coffeehouses made gifts to the crew of the ship that brought the news. Taverns served punch and beer on the house. Benjamin Franklin was once more a hero. Even the Penn supporters had to admit he had done a fine job. At the Philadelphia State House, 300 guests of the governor and the mayor drank a toast to him.

Franklin's own celebration was to go shopping. With Mrs. Stevenson to guide him, he bought more presents for his wife and Sally—fourteen yards of Pompadour satin for a new gown, a silk negligee, a petticoat of "brocaded lutestring," a Turkish carpet, crimson mohair for curtains, three damask tablecloths, and a box of "three fine cheeses."

"Perhaps a bit of them may be left when I come home," he wrote hopefully to Debby.

He had asked the Pennsylvania Assembly to let him come home but instead they appointed him agent for another year.

10
FRIENDSHIPS IN ENGLAND

Some time early in 1766, a young man named Joseph Priestley, a dissenting minister and a teacher of classical languages in Warrington, Lancashire, came to see Franklin to ask his help for a history of electricity he was writing. Franklin gladly gave him assistance and told him of his kite experiment in more detail than he had done to anyone before.

Impressed with Priestley's scientific talents, he recommended him to membership in the Royal Society. Priestley more than fulfilled his expectations. A few years later he would discover oxygen—calling it by the cumbersome name of "dephlogistated air." He also became a lifelong friend of the American colonies.

Inevitably, the most brilliant scientists in England and the continent sought Franklin out and, except for a few jealous ones, were added to the circle of his friendships. Among the most intimate of these was John Pringle, whom he had met on his last English trip and who was now Sir John, personal Physician to England's Queen. Samuel Johnson's biographer, Boswell, once called on Pringle and found him and Franklin playing chess.

Boswell wrote: "Sir John, though a most worthy man, has a peculiar sour manner. Franklin again is all jollity and pleasantry. I said to myself: Here is a prime contrast: acid and alkali."

With Pringle, Franklin took a trip to the continent in June 1766. They stayed first in Pyrmont, in what is now West Germany, a fashionable mineral springs resort. From there they visited Göttingen, where the Royal Society of Sciences elected both to membership. They met Rudolf Erich Raspe, narrator of the famous tall tales of the adventures of Baron Münchausen. In their turn, Pringle and Franklin entertained their new friends with stories about the giant Patagonians of South America, which neither of them had of course ever seen. When Franklin later read the newspaper accounts of their voyage, he noted with amusement that the Patagonians had grown even taller in the hands of the press.

A letter was waiting for him in London from Debby, saying that Sally wanted his consent to marry a young man named Richard Bache. Franklin was too far away to judge the merits of her suitor: "I can only say that if he proves a good husband to her, and a good son to me, he shall find me as good a father as I can be," he wrote. The marriage took place in October 1767. The ships in the harbor in Philadelphia ran up their flags to celebrate the wedding of the daughter of their most famous citizen.

The ministry of Lord Rockingham, in which Franklin had such confidence, toppled while he was in Germany. The King and William Pitt, now Lord Chatham, set up a coalition cabinet. Pitt, still a good friend of the American colonies, soon fell violently ill, during which time the reins of the government were seized by Charles Townshend, chancellor of the exchequer.

Townshend considered the whole colonial uproar over taxes "perfect nonsense." Since the Americans had balked at the *internal* Stamp Tax, he resolved to let them pay *external* taxes, in the form of import duties on glass, lead, paper, paints—and tea.

By the Townshend Acts, duties were to be collected by English revenue officers. The acts violated the time-honored right of trial by jury; those accused of ignoring the revenue laws were to be tried in the admiralty courts without a jury. As an added insult, the revenue collected was to be used for the salaries of royal governors and judges who previously had been paid by the Assemblies and thus subject to some colonial control.

Franklin foresaw grave danger ahead. The Americans would not accept these harsh measures. "Every act of oppression will sour their tempers," he wrote Lord Kames, "lessen greatly—if not annihilate ... the profits of your commerce with them, and hasten their final revolt; for the seeds of liberty are universally found there, and nothing can eradicate them."

He felt that the colonists' affection for Britain was such that "if cultivated prudently" they might be easily governed "without force or any considerable expense." But he did not see "a sufficient quantity of the wisdom that is necessary to produce such a conduct."

The lack of "a sufficient quantity of the wisdom" on the part of Parliament and the ministry was almost daily becoming more obvious to him. Still he continued his course of education and propaganda and persuasion, and of meeting with men in the government whom he hoped to influence. Many listened to him. The young and wealthy Earl of Shelburne, Secretary of State for the Colonies, became his close friend. In recognition of his usefulness to his country, in 1768 he was chosen agent for Georgia; in 1769, for

New Jersey; and in 1770, for Massachusetts.

Nearly every year he took a trip from London for his health and to refresh his mind. In the fall of 1767, he made his first visit to France, again in the company of his "steady, good friend," Sir John Pringle. As a loyal subject of an England frequently at war with France, he was prejudiced in advance against "that intriguing nation," as he called it. Even this first short visit led him to reverse his opinion.

"It seems to be a point settled here universally that strangers are to be treated with respect," he wrote Polly Stevenson. "Why don't we practise this urbanity to Frenchmen? Why should they be allowed to outdo us in anything?" Already he was adopting French fashions. "I had not been here six days before my tailor and peruquier [wig maker] had transformed me into a Frenchman. Only think what a figure I make in a little bag-wig and naked ears! They told me I was become twenty years younger, and looked very *galant*."

In French scientific circles, his name was legendary. Scientists bragged that they were *Franklinistes*, a word they had coined. Thomas d'Alibard, the first to draw electricity from the skies, entertained him royally. At Versailles, he and Sir John were presented to Louis XV, whose praise of his electrical experiments Franklin could hardly have forgotten, and whom he found "a handsome man, has a very lively look, and appears younger than he is."

The King "talked a good deal to Sir John," he wrote Polly, "asking many questions about our royal family; and did me too the honour of taking some notice of me.

That's saying enough, for I would not have you think me so much pleased with this king and queen as to have a whit less regard than I used to have for ours." "Our king" to him was still George III.

He thought Versailles badly kept up in spite of its splendor but was impressed with the way drinking water was kept pure by filtering it through cisterns filled with sand.

It seemed as though every time he turned his back to London there were changes in the ministry. Townshend, who had done more than any man before him to turn the Americans into revolutionists, died in September 1767. He was succeeded by the Tory, Lord North, a pompous thick-lipped personage, who had neither the will nor the desire to improve colonial relations. William Pitt's health was still poor. He collapsed in 1768 in the House of Lords, in the midst of a fiery attack on his government's American policies. In the same year, the pleasant Lord Shelburne was succeeded by the Earl of Hillsborough, a master of hypocrisy in Franklin's estimation, as Secretary of State for the Colonies.

In America, the Massachusetts Assembly sent a letter to other colony assemblies, proposing united opposition to the Townshend Acts. Hillsborough demanded that they rescind their action or dissolve. The Assembly refused, and was backed by the other colonies. In October 1768, the British sent eight ships of war to try to compel Boston to pay the import taxes. Other ships followed. By one estimate the extra military expenses that year were five thousand times the amount which the Townshend Acts produced in revenue. Franklin had judged their stupidity rightly.

In the midst of the American protests against these acts, he was entertained by the Lord Chancellor Lord Bathurst and Lady Bathurst. He brought them a gift of American nuts and apples. With an irony that his lordship could not have missed, he prayed them to accept his present "as a tribute from the country, small indeed but voluntary." The nuts and apples had come from Debby, who also sent him such American products as corn meal, buckwheat flour, cranberries and dried peaches.

That year young Christian VII of Denmark visited England, and insisted that Franklin dine with him at St. James. He would not have been human had he not recalled the proverb of Solomon which his father had so frequently quoted in his childhood. Now he had not only stood before one king, Louis XV, he had sat down with a second. There would be others.

The English tried for two more years to make the colonists pay duties they did not want to pay. At last, on March 5, 1770, Parliament voted unanimously to repeal all of them but the tax on tea. Franklin commented dryly that repealing only part of the duties was as bad surgery as to leave splinters in a wound "which must prevent its healing." In Boston on that same day a squad of British soldiers fired into a crowd which had been pelting them with snowballs—killing five and wounding six. The "Boston Massacre" became a *cause célèbre*. Bloodshed had been added to the other colony grievances.

The next summer Franklin visited Ireland. In Dublin, he attended two sessions of the Irish Parliament. The Speaker introduced him as "an American gentleman of distinguished character and merit," and he was given a place of honor. He noted that the Irish Parliamentarians were more cordial than their English counterparts, but was too astute not to realize they did not really represent their own people. Ireland, like America, had suffered under British oppressive measures, but more intensely and longer. The appalling misery of the Irish people was a moral lesson to him. He foresaw that if the colonists did not continue to insist on their rights, they would suffer the same wretched fate.

Sally's husband, Richard Bache, came to England that fall to meet his famous father-in-law. Bache had set his heart on getting a political appointment and had brought a thousand pounds in case he would have to pay for it. Even members of the House of Commons bought their posts, a practice which was responsible for much of the corruption and inefficiency of the government. Franklin advised his son-in-law to stay clear of politics.

"Invest your money in merchandise. Start a store in Philadelphia. You will be independent and less subject to the caprices of superiors."

Bache followed this advice and within a few years was one of Pennsylvania's most respected merchants.

That year Lord Hillsborough, with whom Franklin's relations had been only outwardly civil, was succeeded by Lord Dartmouth, whom he liked. Again his hopes were raised for a cessation of hostilities. In truth, the ministry and Parliament had never treated him more cordially.

"As to my situation here," he wrote his son on August 19, 1772, "nothing can be more agreeable ... a general respect paid me by the learned, a number of friends and acquaintances among them with whom I have a pleasing intercourse ... my company so much desired that I seldom dine at home in winter and could spend the whole summer in the country houses of inviting friends if I chose it.... The king too has lately been heard to speak of me with great regard." In a postscript he mentioned that the French Royal Academy had chosen him a foreign member, of which there were only eight.

His Craven Street family was now enlarged to include his grandson William Temple Franklin, and a distant English cousin named Sally Franklin who was, like his daughter, an eager young girl "nimble-footed and willing to run errands and wait upon me." Mrs. Stevenson continued to pamper him and nurse him during his spells of gout. Polly, for whom he always had great affection, was married to a young doctor, William Hewson. The young couple had been living with their mother since 1770.

There were several weeks when Mrs. Stevenson was away, leaving Polly in charge. To amuse them, Franklin composed a newspaper, the *Craven Street Gazette*, reporting the daily household happenings as though they were world events. In this sheet, Mrs. Stevenson was "Queen Margaret," Sally was "first maid of honor," Polly and her husband were "Lord and Lady Hewson," while he referred to himself as the "Great Person"—"so called from his enormous size."

When Debby wrote him of the cleverness of his grandson Benjamin Franklin Bache, born in August 1769, Franklin responded with anecdotes about Polly's first boy, whose godfather he was.

Wherever he was, a rich family life was as essential to his happiness as food. Among his close friends was Jonathan Shipley, bishop of St. Asaph, at Twyford. "I now breathe with reluctance the smoke of London, when I think of the sweet air of Twyford," he wrote after a visit there in June 1771.

The bishop had five daughters and a son, and Franklin more or less adopted them all. To the Shipley girls he presented a gray squirrel which Debby had sent. They were thrilled with Skugg, as they named him. One day the squirrel escaped from his cage and was killed by a dog. The children buried him in their garden and Franklin composed his epitaph:

>Here Skugg
>
>Lies snug
>
>As a bug
>
>In a rug.

At the Shipleys he wrote the first part of his famous *Autobiography* in the form of a letter to William.

Another of his intimates was Lord Le Despencer, former chancellor of the exchequer, who in his youth was reputedly the "wickedest man in England." Franklin found him a delightful companion and often stayed at his country place at Wycombe. "I am in this house," he wrote William, "as much at my ease as if it was my own; and the gardens are a paradise. But a pleasanter thing is the kind countenance, the facetious and very intelligent conversation of mine host." With Lord Le Despencer, the alleged "rake," he wrote an *Abridgement of the Book of Common Prayer*, published in 1773.

He was a frequent guest of Lord Shelburne, whose vast wooded estate was also at Wycombe. One windy day he gravely told the other visitors that he could quiet the waves on a small stream on the grounds. Ignoring their skeptical looks, he walked upstream, made some mysterious passes over the water, and waved his cane three times in the air. As he had prophesied, the waves quieted down and the stream became smooth as a mirror. His companions could not conceal their astonishment.

Later he satisfied their curiosity. There was oil in the hollow joint of his cane. A few drops of it spread in a thin film over the water and caused the seeming miracle.

Back of this trick was a great deal of serious study on the effects of pouring oil on troubled waters. In his youth he had read in Pliny how sailors of ancient Greece had smoothed a choppy sea in this manner. On one of his ocean crossings an old sea captain told him that Bermuda fishermen poured oil on rough waters so they could see the fish strike. Subsequently, he had made his own experiments, finding that one teaspoon of oil would calm a pond several yards across.

If such a minute bit of oil would still a pond, would not several barrels of oil level out the surf, making it possible for boats to land with less danger? He tried out this theory the next year at Portsmouth, England. With a local sea captain he took off on a barge one windy day, sprinkling oil on the waves from a large stone bottle. The experiment was only partially successful. Oil did not diminish the height or force of the surf on the shore, but he had the satisfaction of seeing that where the oil had spread, the surface of the water was not wrinkled by smaller waves or whitecaps.

His scientific and cultural interests were as varied as life itself. He was in turn occupied with the nature of mastodon tusks and teeth which a friend sent to London, with the transit of Venus, the causes of lead poisoning, population increase, geology, salt mines, Scottish tunes, whirlwinds and water-spouts, and the science of phonetics—the need of reforms to reduce the "disorderly confusion in English spelling"—and the curious fact that flies apparently drowned in a bottle of Madeira wine might sometimes be brought back to life.

His observations on all these matters were published in *Letters on Philosophical Subjects*, and added to the fourth edition of "Experiments and Observations on Electricity." Barbeu Dubourg, a Parisian printer, issued a French translation in two handsome volumes, which included "The

Way to Wealth," under the French title, "*Le Moyen de s'Enricher.*"

Philadelphia, wrote Dubourg in his preface, was founded in the midst of the savages of America by William Penn, a man wiser than the Spartan hero Lycurgus. In less than a century the city had gone far beyond the ancient world in the practice of the purest virtues and the most useful arts. Benjamin Franklin, scientist, statesman, and sage, had now brought this heroic age to troubled Europe.

The legend of Benjamin Franklin, which would mount to greater heights in France than anywhere else in the world, was already in the making.

11
THE TERRIBLE HUTCHINSON LETTERS

At sixty-seven, Franklin had an expression at once benign, kindly, and humorous. His years in England had subtly altered his appearance and his manner. He dressed with elegance in a smooth wig and fashionable ruffles, and he was equally at ease with eleven-year-old Kitty Shipley or the King's ministers. During the London season, he set out each afternoon in his coach, often with Temple, his lively grandson, to leave his card or pay calls on members of Parliament or other influential persons whom he wished to win over to the American cause.

In the year 1773, he was most concerned with the threat of the British troops still stationed in Boston three years after the "Boston Massacre." Wherever he thought it might help, he argued the folly of treating Bostonians like troublesome children. "I am in perpetual anxiety lest the mad measure of mixing soldiers among a people whose minds are in such a state of irritation, may be attended with some sudden mischief," he wrote his Boston correspondent, Thomas Cushing.

One day, during a conversation on this subject, a British "gentleman of character and distinction" told him that he was wrong to blame the English for the troops in Boston. They had been requested by some of his most respectable fellow countrymen.

Franklin was incredulous. The gentleman then turned over to him some letters written between 1767 and 1769 by two Massachusetts Crown officers, both native Americans, Thomas Hutchinson and Andrew Oliver. In effect, it was as Franklin had been told. Hutchinson, and Oliver too, pleaded of England "a firm hand," even armed forces, to keep order. They demanded for Massachusetts "an abridgment of what are called English liberties."

By the time Franklin read these letters, Oliver was lieutenant governor of Massachusetts and Thomas Hutchinson was governor. Hutchinson had as an excuse that his house had been ransacked during the Stamp Act furor. This did not alter that he had been undermining the work of colonial agents and betraying the very people he had been chosen to govern.

In his position as agent for Massachusetts, Franklin knew he must warn their

Assembly. After some reflection, he sent the letters to Thomas Cushing, asking that they be returned to him after Cushing and members of the Assembly Committee of Correspondence, a small and trusted group, had studied them. He further explained that he could not reveal the source of the letters and that he was not at liberty to make them public. He had no scruples about showing the letters since they were political, not personal, but he had to protect the "gentleman of distinction" who had entrusted them with him.

In due time the letters reached Cushing, who followed Franklin's instructions. Neither Cushing nor anyone else who saw the letters could prevent their being talked about. In June 1773, Samuel Adams, one of the most ardent of Boston patriots, read them to a secret session of the Massachusetts Assembly. Someone took the responsibility of having them copied and printed. In the public uproar that ensued, the Assembly prepared a petition to the King to remove both Hutchinson and Oliver from office.

Perhaps it was for the best, Franklin decided when the news reached him. Without reproaches, he wrote Cushing that he was grateful his own name had not been mentioned, "though I hardly expect it." He only hoped that the letters' publication would not "occasion some riot of mischievous consequence."

He was continuing his own methodical and unrelenting pressure to bring reason to the English government. In September 1773, an anonymous and stinging satire appeared in the *Public Advertiser* under the title "Rules by Which a Great Empire may be Reduced to a Small One." Among the rules cited were:

Forget that their colonies were founded at the expense of the colonists;

Resent their importance to the Empire;

Suppose them always inclined to revolt, and treat them accordingly;

Choose "inferior, rapacious and pettifogging" men for governors and judges in the provinces;—and reward these men for having governed badly.

In all, the "Rules" encompassed every fault and folly of which England was guilty in its treatment of the American colonies. Ministers and members of Parliament could not doubt that the piece came from the quill pen of Benjamin Franklin. It was followed by an even more devastating attack on British policy: "Edict by the King of Prussia."

Frederick the Great of Prussia, the "Edict" announced, was now taking up his claims on the province of Great Britain, which had been settled originally by German colonists and had never been emancipated. Hence the Prussian government had the right to exact revenue from its "British colonies," to lay duties on all goods they exported or imported, to forbid all manufacturing in these "colonies."

From now on, should the British need hats, they must send raw materials to Prussia, which would manufacture the hats and let the British purchase them. (This was exactly the manner in which the British were preventing American manufacture.) Next, Prussia planned to ship to "the island of Great Britain" all the "thieves, highway and street robbers, housebreakers, and murderers" whom they "do not think fit here to hang." (Here Franklin returned to an old grievance—

Britain's using the colonies as a dumping ground for convicts. In 1751 he had proposed tongue-in-cheek to send American rattlesnakes to England in exchange.)

He was visiting Lord Le Despencer when a servant brought to the breakfast table the newspaper which had printed the "Edict" hoax. A fellow guest named Paul Whitehead read the first paragraphs and exploded:

"Here's the King of Prussia claiming a right to this kingdom.... I dare say we shall hear by next post that he is upon his march with one hundred thousand men to back this."

Franklin kept a straight face. Whitehead read on until, as absurdities piled up, it dawned on him that he had been taken:

"I'll be hanged, Franklin, if this is not some of your American jokes upon us."

They admitted he had made his point very cleverly and all had a good laugh.

But neither the "Rules" nor the "Edict" persuaded Parliament and the ministry to change their ways. Colonial resentment focused on the tax on tea, which small as it was, remained a "splinter in the unhealed wound." In Boston, on December 16, 1773, fifty citizens, dressed as Mohawk Indians, defiantly dumped 342 chests of British tea into the ocean. Parliament, when the news reached London, acted swiftly. Until restitution was made for the tea, the port of Boston was to be closed. Four more regiments under General Thomas Gage were sent to keep order. Boston became an occupied city, unable to conduct its commerce and faced with financial ruin.

Pay for the tea, Franklin urged his Boston colleagues. The Boston Tea Party was an act of lawlessness which could only harm the cause of the colonies. Just as the colonists were unaware of the problems that faced him daily in England, so he was too far away to appreciate the fire of indignation that was sweeping America.

In the meantime a scandal had erupted in London as a result of the publication of Governor Hutchinson's letters. Two gentlemen, William Whately and John Temple, had each accused the other of making the letters public. They carried the argument to the newspapers, and then Temple challenged Whately to a duel. It was fought at Hyde Park on December 11, with pistols and swords. Whately was wounded. Neither party was satisfied.

Franklin was out of town when the duel took place. After he heard about it, he realized what he had to do. On Christmas Day, a letter signed by him appeared in the *Public Advertiser*, which said that both Whately and Temple were "ignorant and innocent" of the publication of the Hutchinson letters, that he was the one who had obtained them and sent them to Boston. The entire blame was his. He did not give the name of the man who had turned the letters over to him. This secret he carried to his grave.

How many high-placed persons in England were waiting to get something on this imperturbable Philadelphian! How many resented the way, like Socrates' gadfly, he forced them to admit what they did not want to admit, and pestered them eternally with his troublesome colonies. Now they would have their revenge. Franklin knew his admission would bring wrath on his head. He had not long to wait.

On January 29, 1774, he was summoned to the Cockpit Tavern, to a meeting of the King's Privy Council for Plantation Affairs. The subject given was the petition of the Massachusetts Assembly for the removal from office of Andrew Oliver and Governor Hutchinson. Franklin's friends had informed him already that the petition was to be denied. There were even rumors that his papers might be seized and himself thrown in prison. He was prepared for the worst.

He arrived on time, dressed in a suit of figured Manchester velvet, wearing an old-fashioned curled wig, and carrying the same cane with which he had once quieted the ripples on the stream at Lord Shelburne's estate.

Thirty-six members of the Privy Council were seated around a large table. Among them were the Archbishop of Canterbury, the Bishop of London, the Duke of Queensberry, Lord Dartmouth, whom he had found sympathetic; Lord Hillsborough, who hated and feared him; and the Earl of Sandwich (from whom the word "sandwich" was derived); the London head of the post office, a conceited individual who disliked everything that Franklin stood for. Among them, Franklin could be positive of only one friend—Lord Le Despencer.

A few spectators had been admitted, including Joseph Priestley, the scientist, and Edmund Burke, the Irish peer. They stood behind the table since there were no extra chairs. No one offered Franklin a chair either. For the entire hearing he stood by the fireplace, facing the councilors.

It opened with a reading of the Massachusetts petition and of the Hutchinson and Oliver letters. Franklin's lawyer, John Dunning, appealed to the King's "wisdom and goodness" to favor the petition and remove the two men from their posts, as a gesture to quiet colonial unrest. Then Alexander Wedderburn, lawyer for Hutchinson, took over.

His speech, which lasted an hour, was from beginning to end a tirade against Franklin. Franklin could have got hold of the controversial letters only by fraudulent or corrupt means, he said. His own letter, clearing Whately and Temple of blame, was "impossible to read without horror." Franklin was "a receiver of goods dishonorably come by." He had duped the "innocent, well-meaning farmers" of the Massachusetts Assembly.

Wedderburn's accusations grew wilder as he warmed to his subject. Franklin wanted to become governor himself, he stated categorically. That was why he had taken on himself "to furnish materials for dissensions; to set at variance the different branches of the legislature; and to irritate and incense the minds of the King's subjects against the King's governor."

While Wedderburn continued to spew forth his poisonous invective, Franklin stood stoically, his face impassive, seemingly unaware either of the triumphal smirks of his enemies or the compassionate glances of his friends. People agreed later that his silence, in face of the screams of his adversary, showed him the stronger man. When the hearing was over, he went quietly home alone.

He made no answer to Wedderburn, nor even to those closest to him did he indicate that the attack rankled. To Thomas Cushing he wrote, "Splashes of dirt thrown upon my character I suffered while fresh to remain. I did not choose to spread by endeavouring to remove them, but relied on the vulgar adage that they would all rub off when they were dry."

The day after the hearing he was notified of his dismissal as deputy postmaster-general of the colonies. This was a severe blow, for he had prided himself on the efficient work he had done in this service. Then, on February 7, 1774, the King formally rejected the Massachusetts Assembly petition to remove Hutchinson and Oliver.

Seemingly Franklin's usefulness as a provincial agent was ended. He thought of going home but decided against it. Critical days were ahead. He felt he might still, in spite of his disgrace, find ways of helping his country.

Except that he had no direct dealings with the ministry or Parliament, his life went on as before. He discussed scientific matters with Joseph Priestley, among them the phenomenon of marsh gas. When Polly Hewson's husband died, leaving her with three children, he grieved with and for her. He worried lest William be removed from the governorship of New Jersey as further punishment to him, but this did not happen.

In September 1774, a dark-haired youngish man, who spoke in the Quaker manner, paid him a visit. His name was Thomas Paine, he said. He was fascinated by Franklin's work in electricity and gave evidence of being well informed himself on scientific matters. He had also done a bit of writing, particularly a quite eloquent petition to Parliament on the plight of the excisemen, a petition that had cost him his own job in the excise service.

He had a dream of going to America, Paine confided. Would Dr. Franklin be good enough to give him some advice?

Franklin rarely refused such requests. In this case, he was sufficiently impressed to write a note of recommendation to his son-in-law Richard Bache. He could not guess the enormous favor he was doing his homeland by sending Thomas Paine to America's shores.

Massachusetts had rejected Franklin's advice to pay for the Boston Tea Party. Other colonies were coming to the rescue of beleaguered Boston. Connecticut sent flocks of sheep. From Virginia came flour. South Carolina gave rice. Franklin was delighted; at last the colonies were helping each other, nearly twenty years after he had proposed a union at the Albany conference.

When the First Continental Congress met in Philadelphia in May 1774, he was full of praise for "the coolness, temper, and firmness of the American proceedings," and he was all in favor of a strong boycott of British manufacturers. "If America would save for three or four years the money she spends in fashions and fineries and fopperies of this country she might buy the whole Parliament, ministers and all."

At last his beloved colonies were learning the value of concerted and dignified action, so much more effective, in his thinking, than mob actions.

As the crisis deepened, one by one important statesmen sought him out and almost humbly asked his advice as to what they should do. The great William Pitt summoned him in August. Did he think the colonists would go as far as to ask for independence? Franklin assured him, truthfully, that he "never had heard in any conversation, from any person drunk or sober, the least expression of a wish for a separation or hint that such a thing would be advantageous to America."

He received an invitation to play chess with the sister of Admiral Lord Richard Howe. At their second session, Miss Howe pressed him to tell her what should be done to settle the dispute between Great Britain and the colonies. "They should kiss and be friends," he said lightly. Nor would he be more explicit when she brought Admiral Lord Howe to talk with him. In his heart he knew it was now too late to repair the many blunders on the part of Parliament and the King.

On December 18, 1774, he received the Declaration of Rights and Grievances, a petition from the First Continental Congress to George III. The King, who was having the first of those attacks which would end in insanity, ignored it completely. With William Pitt, Admiral Lord Howe, and other of the more reasonable officials, Franklin spent long hours trying to work out a compromise that would keep the peace. It was all in vain.

In the midst of these labors, word reached him that his faithful Debby had died of a stroke on December 19—the day after the arrival of the petition.

There would be no more of her warm and loving and atrociously spelled letters to keep him informed about his relatives: "I donte know wuther you have bin told that Cosin Benney Mecome and his Lovely wife and five Dafters is come here to live and work Jurney worke I had them to Dine and drink tee yisterday...."

Or to lament the lack of news from him: "I have bin verey much distrest a bout [you] as I did not [get] oney letter nor one word from you nor did I hear one word from oney bodey that you wrote to so I muste submit and indever to submit to what I am to bair."

Letters which she might sign "Your afeckshonet wife," or when she was less careful "Your ffeckshonot wife." He would miss them, but above all he would miss the assurance that she was there waiting for him, loyal and cheerful, to greet him whenever he returned from his long voyage.

He stayed on in England only a few months longer. His last day in London he spent with Joseph Priestley. Together they read papers from America, and now and then tears ran down Franklin's cheeks. He was sure America would win if there were a war, he told Priestley, but it would take at least ten years.

On March 25, 1775, he and his grandson Temple embarked on the *Pennsylvania Packet*. The crossing took six weeks and the weather was pleasant. In the first half of it, he wrote out the complicated story of his recent dealings with the ministry in his last futile and desperate efforts to prevent war. The last part of the journey he devoted to studying the nature of the Gulf Stream, taking its temperature two to four times a day, and noting that its water had a special color of its own and "that it does not sparkle in the night."

Thus he was able to enjoy a brief interlude in the world of nature between the bitter disputes he left behind and the struggle that lay ahead.

12
BEGINNING OF A LONG WAR

He reached Philadelphia on May 5, 1775—an elderly widower, nearly seventy, grave and saddened by the loss of his wife, by the crisis to his country which his many years of negotiations could not forestall. Sally and Richard Bache took him to the house on Market Street which he had designed but never occupied. Two small grandchildren whom he had never seen, Benjamin and William Bache, were waiting to embrace him and to greet their youthful English cousin, Temple. Franklin's friends of the Junto and political companions were on hand to give him the big news.

On April 19, while he was on the high seas, that was when it had happened. General Sir William Howe (another brother of the chess-playing Miss Howe), who was now stationed in Boston, had sent some 800 British soldiers to Concord, where the Massachusetts Committee of Safety had a store of arms and ammunition. The Massachusetts Minutemen, forewarned by Paul Revere, had tried to stop them at Lexington. The Redcoats, who claimed that the colonials fired first, had killed eight and left ten wounded, then pushed onwards. It was at Concord where for the first time in America the King's subjects shot at the King's troops. The return of the Redcoats was a rout, with farmers and tradesmen firing behind every barn and haystack. General Howe announced 73 of his men slain and 174 wounded.

A rebellion was under way and there was no turning back.

On his second day home, Franklin was chosen as a Pennsylvania delegate to the Second Continental Congress. It opened on May 10 in the Philadelphia State House; delegates from all the colonies attended. In both years and experience, Franklin was the senior member.

Colonel George Washington, a big quiet man of forty-three, wore his colonial uniform, as if guessing the heavy responsibility ahead of him as Commander-in-Chief of the Continental Armies. On the day he left for Cambridge to assume his post, word came of the valiant fight at Breed Hill (which history would call the Battle of Bunker Hill). Another tall Virginian joined the Congress, red-haired Thomas Jefferson, thirty-two years old, lawyer and college graduate and of a wealthy and cultured family. In spite of differences in age and background, Franklin found him a kindred spirit. Jefferson, like himself, was a scientist, inventor, man of letters.

In July, Congress voted to send another petition to their "gracious sovereign," asking for a redress of grievances. Franklin knew in advance that this "olive branch" petition was a waste of paper, but he did not voice his objections. Let these impulsive young men of Congress find out for themselves that the weak and stubborn George III was not on their side. They would likely not have taken his word anyway.

In sessions of Congress he spoke less than any man present. In his school days he had learned a jingle: "A man of words and not of deeds / Is like a garden full of weeds." Better to show one's patriotism in action than talk.

Congress did its work largely by committees. Franklin served on a committee for the making of paper money, on committees to protect colony trade, to investigate lead ore deposits, and to study the cheapest and easiest way to procure salt. He was on another committee which considered, and turned down, a reconciliation plan submitted by Lord North. He was one of three commissioners appointed to handle Indian affairs in Pennsylvania and Virginia.

On July 25, the Congress voted him postmaster-general of the colonies. The postal system which he set up with his son-in-law Richard Bache was so efficient and comprehensive that it served as a model to modern times, giving Franklin right to the title, "Father of the American Post Office."

For local defense, the Pennsylvania Assembly set up a Committee of Safety, appointing Franklin as president. Among his duties were the reorganizing of the Philadelphia militia, selecting officers for armed boats, obtaining medicines for the soldiers. He designed a special pike—a long wooden pole with pointed metal head—to be used in hand-to-hand fighting as a substitute for bayonets, which the colonists did not have. Half-seriously, he proposed use of bows and arrows, in lieu of more powerful weapons. To keep British warships from coming within firing range of Philadelphia, he had built huge contraptions of logs and iron, called *Chevaux de Frise*, to be sunk in the Delaware River.

On his papers and plans he worked late night after night. He met with the

Committee of Safety at six each morning. From nine to four he sat in Congress. It was small wonder that delegate John Adams would catch him napping during the hot and often wearisome sessions. No one knows how he found time for his postmaster duties.

Could anything more be expected of old Ben Franklin who twenty-eight years before had decided to retire, since he had enough money to live on, and no man needed more than enough? In all those years he had continued to work for his city, his province, the thirteen colonies. His greatest services still lay ahead.

He was sure America would win—eventually. He had no illusions about the hardships involved. England was the most powerful country in the world, swollen with the glory of its victories over France and Spain. Its superb navy was rivaled by none. Its army was well-trained, well-armed, disciplined, and numerous. The Americans had to start from scratch.

The embargo against English goods had boomeranged sadly. America was still an agricultural country with little manufacturing of its own. There were shortages of necessities and of luxuries. That year Abigail Adams sent a tearful request to her husband, John, to buy her a box of pins in Philadelphia—even if it cost ten dollars.

The most urgent need was for arms and ammunition. From General Washington at Cambridge came letter after letter, pleading for them. One note, confessing that he had no more than half a pound of gunpowder per soldier, fell into the hands of General Howe—who thought it was a trick. (It was not until March 1776 that Henry Knox brought down guns captured at Ticonderoga and Washington could frighten Howe and his troops from Boston.)

One of Franklin's many Congressional committees was formed to promote the manufacture of saltpeter for gunpowder. Progress was slow. Throughout the war, the colonies produced only about fifty tons of gunpowder. Obviously home manufacture was not the answer.

In July, Congress had a visitor from Bermuda, Colonel Henry Tucker, who headed the island's local militia. Tucker was sympathetic to the Americans as were many Bermudians. There was for a time talk of Bermuda being the fourteenth colony to revolt against British domination. It had previously been dependent on America for foodstuffs, but as it was a British possession shipments had been stopped. Colonel Tucker had come to plead that the ban be lifted.

Franklin found occasion to talk with Tucker privately and one thing the Bermudian told him interested him greatly. At the Royal Arsenal at St. George, there was a large stock of gunpowder—and no guard.

On Franklin's recommendation, Congress put through a blanket order to exchange food for guns with any vessel arriving on the American coast, an order which evaded the controversial point of trading with an enemy. Bermuda was promised not only food, but candles, soap and lumber. There was another deal with Colonel Tucker, about which only those intimately concerned were informed.

In August, two ships set sail for Bermuda—the *Lady Catherine* from Virginia and the *Savannah Pacquet* from South Carolina. At Mangrove Bay, their crews disembarked, to be welcomed by friendly Bermudians, including the son of

Colonel Tucker. Bermudians and American seamen boarded small boats and sailed along the coast to St. George, where, on the estate of Bermuda's Governor James Bruere, the Royal Arsenal was located.

The raiders waited until the governor, his fourteen children, and his numerous watchdogs were all asleep. They proceeded so stealthily that not even a dog was wakened. A sailor, lowered into the arsenal through a vent in the roof, unlocked the doors from inside. Barrels of powder were rolled to the waiting boats. Then the party took off.

Twelve days later the *Lady Catherine* arrived at Philadelphia with 1,800 pounds of gunpowder, while the *Savannah Pacquet* delivered its cargo at Charleston.

This was Franklin's first victory in his battle for ammunition. Although Governor Bruere, on discovering his loss, promptly sent for British warships to patrol the island, Bermudian sloops continued to get through to America, and American ships managed regularly to maneuver around the patrol. The trade continued for the benefit of both Americans and Bermudians.

In the midst of this hectic summer, Franklin spent one long and miserable evening with William, the son whom he had made part of his life as much as any father ever had. He had hoped his flesh and blood would share his burning indignation at English oppression. The most bitter disillusion of his life now faced him. The governor of New Jersey haughtily denied any sympathy for the "American rabble." His loyalty was to the Crown, and that was that.

Franklin continued to write affectionately to Temple, who had gone to stay with his father, but the breach between him and his first-born son remained deep.

The Bermuda raid was Franklin's first step toward a larger plan. The Secret Committee to further importation of war supplies was set up on September 18, 1775. Among those serving with him was Robert Morris, the prosperous merchant who became the financial genius of the American Revolution. The Committee was granted substantial sums of money and wide powers. It made contracts with American merchants who, with permits issued by Congress, took cargoes to the West Indies, Martinique, Santo Domingo, and even Europe, bringing back arms and ammunition.

Part of the Committee's work was to get in touch with merchants from many countries. England was no exception. The friendships Franklin had formed among English merchants when he was seeking repeal of the Stamp Act now proved their value. These merchants knew they could trust him and were not adverse to giving a helping hand to the Americans and making a profit at the same time.

There was in the West Indies a tiny island no more than seven or eight miles square called St. Eustatius, a dependency of Holland and an international free port. Statia, as the Americans called it, had long been a market for smuggled goods from every corner of the globe. Now it became an arsenal to which merchants from Holland, France, England, and other nations brought war materials to be picked up by American vessels. The British government, through its excellent espionage system, knew what was happening but could not prevent it.

"Powder cruises," these ventures were called. They were only one phase of American sea activity. There was in time a Continental Navy, which was never very effective. Individual colonies had their own navies. There were also the romantic privateers, privately owned vessels with commissions from Congress, which by the first twenty months of the war had captured over 700 English vessels—and made fortunes for their owners and crews. The powder cruises alone were planned for the sole purpose of getting war materials for the fighting forces.

They were a long-range project. It took time to fit and man and load the ships, more time for them to make their journeys and return. Not for two years would the Americans have enough ammunition to win a major engagement.

Before this happened, there were hard days ahead.

On October 4, Franklin rode off to visit Washington's camp at Cambridge, on a Congressional mission with Thomas Lynch of South Carolina and Benjamin Harrison of Virginia. If he was a little flabbergasted at the motley assembly of backwoodsmen, farmers and teenage youths to whom Washington was trying to teach military discipline, he did not say so. These were his people. He was proud of them and what they had set out to do.

On his return, he stopped in Warwick, Rhode Island, where his sister Jane Mecom, an old woman now, had taken refuge from British-occupied Boston with their old friends, the Greenes. Besides himself, she was the only one of Josiah Franklin's seventeen children who was still living. Happily, she did not yet know that her Boston home was being looted in her absence.

"Sorrows roll over me like the waves of the sea," she had written Franklin a few years before on the death of her adored daughter Polly. She was worried now about her son Benjamin, who was unable to hold a job and whose wife and children were destitute (the same whom Debby had written her husband that she had had to tea). Only a few months later, his mind completely gone, Benjamin wandered out in the dark, never to be seen again.

In spite of the repeated blows of a cruel fate, Jane had remained warmhearted and thoughtful. Franklin, who had the tenderest affection for her, brought her back to Philadelphia, where she stayed with him for the next year. Always he had humored her, given her and her inevitably needy family material help, written her long and loving letters—and occasionally fretted at her constant solicitude.

On this same trip he distributed a hundred pounds, sent by English friends to aid the wounded of Lexington and Concord and the widows and orphans of those who had been killed. It is possible that one of the generous donors was Joseph Priestley, to whom Franklin wrote about this time:

"Britain, at the expense of three millions, has killed one hundred and fifty Yankees in this campaign, which is twenty thousand pounds a head.... During the same time sixty thousand children have been born in America."

His letter was quoted throughout England, where the hearts of many lay not with their own corrupt Parliament, but with those who had the courage to oppose it.

13
THE SPLENDID WORD INDEPENDENCE

As Franklin had foreseen, the King paid no heed to the "olive branch" petition of the Second Continental Congress. By Royal proclamation all Americans were declared Rebels. The British had burned Charlestown in June and Falmouth in October 1775. It was hinted they were buying mercenaries from German princes. That foreigners should be paid by the English to kill English subjects seemed the greatest insult of all.

Franklin composed a short letter to William Strahan, his English printer friend:

MR. STRAHAN:

You are a member of Parliament, and one of that majority which has doomed my country to destruction. You have begun to burn our towns and murder our people. Look upon your hands! They are stained with the blood of your relations. You and I were long friends. You are now my enemy, and I am

Yours,

B. FRANKLIN.

He did not send this cruel note, but instead wrote Strahan a warm and cordial letter which Strahan answered in kind. Perhaps he had written the first one to see how it sounded and when he read it over did not like it. Throughout the conflict he found ways of carrying on a correspondence with those he cherished in England.

On November 29, 1775, the Congressional Committee of Secret Correspondence was formed with five members—Benjamin Franklin and John Dickinson of Pennsylvania, Benjamin Harrison of Virginia, Thomas Johnson of Maryland, and John Jay of New York. Its assignment was to establish closer relations with foreign nations, and where possible to make allies of those nations. With these duties, the Committee of Secret Correspondence became the predecessor of the United States Department of State.

As a member of the new committee, Franklin wrote his friend Charles Dumas, a Swiss journalist with many political connections: "We wish to know whether, if, as seems likely to happen, we should be obliged to break off all connection with

Britain, and declare ourselves an independent people, there is any state or power in Europe, who would be willing to enter into an alliance with us for the benefits of our commerce." In a similar vein he sounded out Barbeu Dubourg, his Paris printer, who had, as he knew, friends high in the French government.

The French were already watching America with interest. The harsh terms of the 1763 treaty with Great Britain still rankled. They welcomed any struggle that would involve England's military forces, particularly if it could be prolonged to seriously weaken her.

In December 1775, a certain Monsieur Achard de Bonvouloir, allegedly an Antwerp merchant, arrived in Philadelphia. Through a French bookseller he arranged to meet Franklin, to whom he admitted that he had connections at the Court of Versailles. In truth he was a French agent, sent by Louis XVI's foreign minister, Count Charles Gravier de Vergennes, to appraise the American situation.

Franklin arranged for Bonvouloir to meet with the Committee of Secret Correspondence at a quiet house in the outskirts of Philadelphia. It turned out to be a very crucial meeting. The French government did not object to American ships coming into her ports to pick up cargoes, Bonvouloir said. If the British complained of the presence of these ships as a breach of neutrality, the government would simply plead ignorance of what was going on. But in return for this welcome assurance of free trade, the French wanted to make sure that America intended to declare its independence from England.

Independence was a word as yet heard rarely. Though Franklin had mentioned its possibility in his letter to Dumas, he knew that few other members of Congress, much less the American people, were ready for such a drastic step. The urgent need for French cooperation made him speak out boldly.

Certainly the Americans were going to separate from England, he told Bonvouloir blandly. The country was behind the war to a man. Everything was going splendidly. General Washington's army was growing.

There was exaggeration in his statements. Not only was talk of independence rare, but America was peppered with Loyalists, those who, like Franklin's own son, were opposed to action against the British Crown. While new recruits were joining Washington, many simply walked off when their time of service was up, and some were deserting outright. But Franklin's words were a magnificent prophecy. He was speaking from his own profound faith in his countrymen, and his confidence was contagious. Bonvouloir sent back a glowing report to the French minister Vergennes; France's secret alliance with America began from that time.

If Americans were not more solidly behind the rebellion, it was that their emotions had not been deeply aroused. Was not the chief dispute a matter of taxes? No one likes to pay taxes, but though people were ready to parade and protest against them, not all were willing to risk their lives rather than pay them. It took the protégé of Franklin, Thomas Paine, to point out that the rebellion was for something much more important than taxes.

Paine had settled in Philadelphia, taken a job with the *Pennsylvania Magazine*, and had, in the few months he had been in America, written some fine articles, among them one of the first attacks on slavery to appear in the American press. Franklin saw him in October and proposed that he write "a history of the present transactions," an account of events that had led to the present crisis. Paine had only looked mysterious, saying that he was working on something.

Then in January 1776, Franklin received the first copy off the press of a pamphlet titled "Common Sense." Though it was published anonymously, "written by an Englishman," he guessed easily who had written it.

"Common Sense," written simply and clearly, was a passioned and reasoned plea for secession from England. It showed Americans how much they had to gain from independence and how little there was to lose. It made them hold up their heads with the pride of being American and convinced them they were fighting for the most precious thing in the world—their freedom. There is no estimating the enormous service done by "Common Sense" in uniting the colonies in a common cause.

In February, Franklin sent in his resignation to the Pennsylvania Assembly and its Committee of Safety: "Aged as I am, I feel myself unequal to do so much business...." At the same time he accepted another arduous assignment from Congress, to head a delegation to Canada to try and win French Canadians to the side of the colonies.

Two expeditions had already been sent to wrest Quebec from the British, one under General Richard Montgomery, the other under Colonel Benedict Arnold. Both had failed. Montgomery had been killed. Arnold, severely wounded, had retreated with his battered army to Montreal.

Franklin, aged seventy, set out on his mission the last week of March 1776. There were stops in New York, Albany, and in Saratoga where the snow was still six inches deep. From there they rode horseback across to the Hudson and proceeded up the river in rowboats to Fort Edward. "I began to apprehend that I have undertaken a fatigue that at my time of life may prove too much for me," Franklin wrote Josiah Quincy.

They sailed along the coast of Lake George in open flatboats, fighting their way through ice. When the cold grew too bitter, they stopped to make fires, thaw out, and brew tea. By April 25 they had reached Lake Champlain, and in clumsy wagons drove over bad roads to the St. Lawrence, where they again took to boats. Their hard journey ended at Montreal on the 29th. Benedict Arnold, now a general, came to meet them, and there was a cannon salute to the "Committee of the Honourable Continental Congress," and to the "celebrated Dr. Franklin."

The conferences the next day proved what Franklin had doubtless suspected. The Canadians for the most part found British rule preferable to French rule and were not dissatisfied. The majority were Catholic and as such hostile to the colonies because of unpleasant things that had been said about their faith.

General Arnold and his men were penniless. Franklin loaned them about 350 pounds of his own money in gold. On May 6, word came that the British were sending reinforcements from England. Franklin guessed that the Americans would be driven from Canada; it happened just a month later. He stayed on until May 11, then, realizing nothing more could be done, set out for home.

He was in New York by the 27th, as worn out and ill as though the vain mission had drained the last bit of his strength. His health returned slowly. From Philadelphia, on June 21, he wrote Washington that gout had kept him from "Congress and company"—that he knew little of what had passed except that "a declaration of independence was in the making."

To this development, the magic of "Common Sense" deserved credit. On April 12, North Carolina had instructed its delegates to Congress to vote for independence. Other colonies followed suit. On June 7, Richard Henry Lee introduced a resolution that "these colonies are, and of a right ought to be, free and independent states." Three days later Congress appointed Thomas Jefferson, John Adams, Robert Livingston of New York, Roger Sherman of Connecticut, and Benjamin Franklin, as a committee to prepare the declaration.

Jefferson produced the first draft. John Adams and Franklin made only a few alterations before it was submitted to Congress on June 18.

Congress nearly drove the Committee out of its mind with demands for extensive changes. One clause which attacked slavery was deleted altogether. When nerves grew tense, Franklin told a story.

There was a hatter he had once known who built a handsome signboard reading, "John Thompson, hatter, makes and sells hats for some ready money," adorned with a picture of a hat. He submitted it to his friends for approval. One thought the word "hatter" unnecessary. Another that "makes" was not needed. A third thought "for ready money" useless, since no one then sold for credit. His next friend insisted "sells hats" be omitted; no one expected him to give them away. All that was left, when his friends were through with him, was his name "John Thompson" and the drawing of the hat.

The moral lesson implied may have speeded up the Congressional process. At length, the Declaration met with approval. John Hancock, in big black writing, affixed his signature first. According to legend, Hancock said, "We must be unanimous; there must be no pulling different ways; we must all hang together." To which Franklin allegedly replied, "We must indeed all hang together, or most assuredly we shall all hang separately."

The ideas in the Declaration were not new. Many of them had been said by others, specifically by Thomas Paine, in phraseology not too different from Jefferson's. The document, adopted by Congress on July 4, 1776, remained the greatest charter of freedom of all time.

In the midst of the wonder of independence, the New Jersey Assembly ordered the arrest of its governor, William Franklin, as a Loyalist, another sad blow for his father. He was first held under guard at his home, then taken to Connecticut, where he was kept for two years in the Litchfield jail or on parole. Temple came to live with his grandfather, attending the Pennsylvania Academy which Franklin had started so many years before.

The Declaration of Independence, splendid as it was, still was only words on paper. The reality was far in the future and the present looked very dark.

On and around Long Island was gathered the greatest British expeditionary force in history. Some 32,000 men (including German mercenaries whom the Americans called Hessians) and 500 vessels were there in command of General Sir William Howe who, after leaving Boston, had gone to Halifax for reinforcements. And in the harbor, a mighty fleet under his brother Admiral Lord Richard Howe. And in Manhattan, General George Washington with less than half as many men, ill-clad and hungry and a good portion too sick to fight.

To get a foothold on Long Island, Washington took half his army to Brooklyn Heights. The results were disastrous—a surprise attack by the British on August 27, brought American casualties, killed and wounded, to nearly two thousand. It was to the credit of Washington, and John Glover's Marbleheaders and former Salem sailors, that boats were found to carry the survivors back to Manhattan under the cloak of night.

Why did not the Howe brothers pursue them then and there? They needed only to send a force up the Hudson or Long Island Sound to trap the Rebels and cut to pieces America's principal army. Yet they dawdled a while. Why?

The truth was that Admiral Lord Howe, whom Franklin had first met at the home of his sister, had come in a dual role of warrior and peace ambassador. He was empowered to offer full pardon to all Rebels (with the secret exception of John Adams) and on his arrival had sent Franklin a flattering and friendly letter making a proposal for reconciliation—which Franklin, with the sanction of Congress, had turned down in an equally cordial missive.

Soon after the Battle of Long Island, Lord Howe sent another request to Philadelphia, by a paroled prisoner, General John Sullivan, for delegates to come and discuss a settlement of hostilities. Franklin, John Adams, and Edward Rutledge of South Carolina were chosen. They met Lord Howe and his staff on September 11, at a neglected house on Staten Island, in a room hung with moss and branches. Americans and British dined on cold ham, tongue, mutton, bread, and claret, all the while making polite conversation. Then they got to business. Lord Howe did most of the talking.

He felt for America as for a brother, he said, and should lament, as a brother, should America fall.

"My Lord, we will use our utmost endeavors to save your lordship that mortification," Franklin said with a guileless smile.

"The King's most earnest desire" was to make his American subjects happy, Howe continued. They would redress any real grievances. It was not money they wanted. America's solid advantage to Great Britain was "her commerce, her strength, her men."

"Aye, my Lord," Franklin said, chuckling, "we have a pretty considerable manufactory of men." He was referring not, as Howe's secretary presumed, to the growing army, but to America's rapidly increasing population.

Howe continued to plead for a resumption of the old relationship with England. Franklin told him firmly that was impossible. Had not their defenseless towns been burned in the midst of winter, Indians encouraged to massacre their farmers, and slaves to murder their masters—and now foreign mercenaries brought to deluge their settlements with blood? Ah no, after these atrocious injuries, there could be no return to their previous status.

The conference ended on this impasse.

Following this meeting, the British drove Washington north to Harlem Heights and on to White Plains. During the evacuation, New York caught fire and a third of it burned. No one ever knew who was responsible. The situation looked hopeless—unless substantial aid could be had from outside. And where could they go for such aid if not to France?

Congress chose three commissioners to represent America at the French court—Jefferson, Franklin, and Silas Deane of

Connecticut, who was already in Paris. When Jefferson declined because of his wife's health, Arthur Lee, cousin of "Light-Horse Harry" Lee of Virginia, was chosen in his place.

Before he left, Franklin appointed Richard Bache as deputy postmaster and turned over to Congress all the money he could raise as a loan—around 4,000 pounds. To his friend Joseph Galloway, he entrusted his trunk, containing his correspondence from the years he had spent in England, as well as the only existing manuscript of his *Autobiography*. He took with him two grandsons, eighteen-year-old Temple Franklin, and Benjamin Franklin Bache, age seven. They left on the sloop *Reprisal*, October 27, 1776.

Did the two youths know what a perilous journey they were making, with the English Navy prowling the seas in search of just such prizes as the *Reprisal*? Temple at least must have realized that if they were captured, his gray-haired grandfather would be considered a prize more valuable than any ship, and would certainly be hanged as a traitor. Not only was the crossing made safely but within two days of landing, the passengers had the thrill of witnessing their captain take two British "prizes," which the *Reprisal* on December 3 brought to Auray on the coast of Brittany.

14

FRANCE FALLS IN LOVE WITH AN AMERICAN

"The carriage was a miserable one," Franklin wrote of the trip from Auray to the French town of Nantes, where the *Reprisal* would have brought them had it not been for the two prizes. "With tired horses, the evening dark, scarce a traveler but ourselves on the road; and, to make it more comfortable, the driver stopped near a wood we were to pass through, to tell us that a gang of eighteen robbers infested that wood who but two weeks ago had murdered some travelers on that very spot."

The Nantes townspeople were expecting the celebrated American and were waiting to greet him as he descended from his carriage.

Instead of a curled and powdered wig, he wore a fur cap over his thin gray straight hair, which he had adopted on shipboard for reasons of comfort. His costume was of brown homespun worsted, with white stockings and buckled shoes. He wore spectacles, because at seventy vanity was less important to him than seeing clearly. He carried a plain crabtree cane, such as any man could have cut for himself.

"A *primitive!*" people exclaimed. His simple attire delighted them all.

For his few days in Nantes he stayed with a commercial agent, Monsieur Gruet. A string of visitors appeared afternoon and evenings to pay their respects. He spoke little, knowing his French was imperfect, and his silence made him seem all the wiser. Everyone was filled with admiration. The women of the town paid him their greatest tribute in a *Coiffure à la Franklin*, dressing their hair in a high curly mass to resemble his fur cap.

His welcome at Nantes was only a preview of what attended him in Paris. His printer, Barbeu Dubourg, had prepared the populace by distributing circulars about his visit. For two days before his arrival, he was the sole subject of conversation in Paris cafés. Wherever he went, admiring citizens surrounded him, remarking on the simplicity of his costume and his unaffected manners. Silas Deane, who had received no such attention on his arrival, was amazed. But then, Deane had little love for the French people, had made no effort to learn their language, and was obviously unhappy in this foreign environment.

From Deane, Franklin learned of a plan already under way to help America. A dummy exporting house had been set up under the name of Hortalez and Company, to which the French and Spanish governments had each contributed a million livres. (The livre is replaced by the franc in modern French currency.) When Deane had reached Paris a few months before, authorized to buy supplies, Foreign Minister Vergennes had promptly sent him to the head of Hortalez, a dashing adventurer named Caron de Beaumarchais (who would later become known for his librettos of *The Marriage of Figaro* and *The Barber of Séville*). The company was now arranging to send arms and ammunition, uniforms, everything the colonies needed.

Since this was Deane's project, Franklin did not interfere. Later, when Americans found they were receiving inferior goods from Hortalez, when Congress was billed for what they were told was a gift, when Beaumarchais unaccountably became wealthy, and even Deane was accused of dishonesty, he may have wished that he had kept a closer check. For the moment, he had plenty of other work to do.

Silas Deane as well as Arthur Lee, the third commissioner, both gave him advice on how to conduct himself. Deane, a blunt and tactless man, was all for forcing the issue with France. Arthur Lee, who had an intriguing nature, advocated a devious approach. Franklin listened attentively to both of them and went his own way.

On December 28, he and Deane were received at Versailles by Vergennes, of whom Franklin had already heard so much. As usual, he wore his brown worsted suit and his head was bare, with no wig to hide his gray locks. Though he did little more than transmit expressions of good will and gratitude from his country, the suave and polished French diplomat summed him up as a great and good man. Henceforth, whenever possible, Vergennes avoided dealing with any American other than Benjamin Franklin.

The next night he attended a soiree held by Madame la Marquise du Deffand. Her guests were the most important personages in Europe. The Marquise was known to be strongly pro-British. Everyone expected that Monsieur Franklin from Philadelphia would be put in his place. How could he compete in this brilliant company? He was much too clever to try. All evening he sat quietly smiling, waiting for others to do the talking, listening with interest to everything that was said, even by the ladies. The company was enchanted. They had believed all Americans to be bold and rude-mannered and self-assertive. This Monsieur Franklin, who dressed like a Quaker, was a sage, a patriarch! They had never known anyone like him. From then on, the aristocracy gave him their adoration, as did the scientific world and the common people.

A few days later there was a gift of two million livres, not connected with the funds at Hortalez, presented for the American cause in the name of the French King. Franklin had, without resort to bullying or conniving, scored his first victory in French diplomacy.

For fear of British retaliation, Vergennes dared not openly sponsor him. Privately he was doing all in his power to convince Louis XVI that the American rebellion, even though against another king, should be supported to the hilt. This was not easy, for the French ruler was not yet ready to show more than a token interest in the Americans. Franklin understood Vergennes' position and did not press him for what he had really come to get, an open alliance. His most important task, from Vergennes' viewpoint, was to win French public opinion to his side. This he did without half trying.

His popularity mounted daily. For the French he was a man of reason, like their Voltaire, and an advocate of the equality of man and the virtues of rustic living, like their philosopher Jean Jacques Rousseau. They saw him as the man who had singlehandedly fomented the American Revolution, a rumor carefully nourished by the British Ambassador in Paris, Lord Stormont.

He was given credit for the Declaration of Independence and the Pennsylvania Constitution. Not knowing yet of Thomas Paine, people took it for granted that he was the author of that marvelous pamphlet "Common Sense," which was reprinted in French with the omission of its attacks on royalty. They admired him alike for his scientific achievements and for "The Way of Wealth," the proverbs of Poor Richard as cited by Father Abraham, which they praised to the skies as "sublime morality."

It became the fashion of every home to have an engraving of him above the mantel. Medallions with his image in enamel adorned the lids of snuffboxes, and tiny ones were even set in rings, selling in incredible numbers. In time his portrait was reproduced on watches, clocks, vases, dishes, handkerchiefs, pocket knives. There were paintings of him without end, and busts in marble, bronze and plaster. "These," Franklin wrote to his daughter Sally, "with the pictures, busts, and prints (of which copies upon copies are spread everywhere), have made your father's face as well known as that of the moon."

The first of March he moved from the Paris hotel where he and his grandsons had been staying to Passy, a beautiful spot half a mile from Paris, less a village than a group of villas set amidst forests and vineyards. Their house was on the great estate of Le Ray de Chaumont, an ardent partisan of the United States, who refused to accept rent from his distinguished guest.

The grounds of the Chaumont estate were laid out in formal gardens around an octagonal pond, with alleys of linden trees. Often Franklin and his grandsons ate at the lavish Chaumont table, or had their meals sent from the Chaumont kitchen for a minimum charge. When he gave a large dinner party in his own quarters, everything would be sent over by the Chaumont staff. He had his own servants, including a coachman, and kept a carriage and a pair of horses. Benjamin Bache went to boarding school in the village, coming home for Sunday. Temple acted as his secretary.

The British, who had spies everywhere, were well aware of the reason for his presence in France. Vainly did British Ambassador Lord Stormont try to belittle him or his country. He could not match Franklin's wit. Once Franklin learned that Stormont was spreading a rumor that 4,000 Americans had been lost in a battle and their general killed. "Truth is one thing. Stormont is another," he commented dryly. In Parisian slang, the verb "to Stormont" became a synonym for "to lie."

In truth, with the exception of Washington's victory over the Hessians at Trenton, the Christmas of 1776, news from America was discouraging. Franklin refused to show any sign of worry. "*Ça ira,*"—"it will go on"—he would say to anyone who asked how the American Revolution was faring. In the years of France's own revolution, Franklin's famous *Ça ira* became the catchword of a popular war song.

Some time that summer, or so it is said, Franklin passed a night at the same inn as Edward Gibbon, author of *Rise and Fall of the Roman Empire*. Franklin sent up a note requesting the pleasure of his company. Gibbon answered that though he admired Franklin as a philosopher he could not, as a loyal English subject, converse with a Rebel. Franklin promptly sent him a second note. He had the greatest respect for the historian, he wrote, and when Gibbon decided to write the *Rise and Fall of the British Empire*, he would be happy to supply all the needed data.

The revolt in America had enormous glamour for innumerable European officers who were eager to offer their services, for money, for the thrill of adventure, and perhaps less often because they believed in the American cause. Franklin was besieged with their requests for him to recommend them to the American army. "My perpetual torment," he called them:

People will believe, notwithstanding my continually repeated declaration to the contrary, that I am sent hither to engage officers. You have no conception how I am harassed.... Great officers of all ranks, in all departments; ladies, great and small, besides professed solicitors, worry me from morning to night.... I am afraid to accept an invitation to dine abroad, being almost sure of meeting some officer or some officer's friend who, as soon as I am put in good humour with a glass of champagne, begins his attack upon me.

Only partly in jest, he composed a form letter:

The bearer of this, who is going to America, presses me to give him a letter of recommendation, though I know nothing of him, not even his name. This may seem extraordinary, but I assure you is not uncommon here. Sometimes, indeed, one unknown person brings another, equally unknown, to recommend him; and sometimes they recommend one another. As to this gentleman, I must refer you to himself for his character and merits, with which he is certainly better acquainted than I can possibly be. I recommend him, however, to those civilities which every stranger of whom one knows no harm has a right to; and I request you will do him all the good offices, and show him all the favour, that on further acquaintance you shall find him to deserve.

Temple later claimed that he actually used this letter on occasion, though it has never been proved.

There was, however, one officer whom Franklin recommended to George Washington without ever having met. This was the nineteen-year-old Marquis de Lafayette, an ardent youth set on revenging a father killed by the English. "He is exceedingly beloved," he wrote Washington early in August after Lafayette had already left France, "and everybody's good wishes attend him; we cannot but hope he may meet with such a reception as will make the country and his expedition agreeable to him."

Another valuable recruit Franklin sent to America was the former Prussian officer

Baron von Steuben, whose rigid training of American troops at Valley Forge raised morale at a moment when it had sunk to a new low.

In England, he still had friends in high places. Lord Rockingham was praising his courage in crossing the Atlantic, risking capture and being brought to an "implacable tribunal." Charles James Fox, a member of Lord North's cabinet, was quoting to his fellow cabinet members Franklin's remark that England's war on America would be as costly and useless as the Crusades. While to George III he had become "that insidious man from Philadelphia," Sir John Pringle, now president of the Royal Society, supported him in one of the few comic episodes of wartime.

During Franklin's stay in England, he had given advice on installing lightning rods on St. Paul's Cathedral and other important buildings. One member of the Royal Society, Benjamin Wilson, an artist who had painted Franklin's portrait, argued that blunt lightning rods would be more effective than pointed ones, but he had been over-ruled. The battle between "the sharps and the flats" raged briefly and then subsided.

It was revived when the war was under way by George III, who felt that since pointed lightning rods had been invented by a Rebel, they must certainly be subversive. He ordered that the rods on his palace and throughout the United Kingdom be replaced by the blunt type and commanded Sir John Pringle to back him. Sir John boldly retorted that the laws of nature were not changeable at royal pleasure. He was thereupon informed that the royal authority did not believe that a man of his views should occupy the presidency of the Royal Society. Sir John, loyal to Franklin to the end, promptly resigned.

As for Franklin, he remained an objective observer: "I have never entered into any controversy in defense of my philosophical opinions," he wrote in October 1777. "I leave them to take their chances in the world. If they are *right*, truth and experience will support them; if *wrong*, they ought to be refuted and rejected. Disputes are apt to sour one's temper, and disturb one's quiet."

In November a visitor to Passy informed him that General Howe had taken Philadelphia. (Congress had fled to York, Pennsylvania, which became temporarily the capital of the United States.) Calm and smiling, Franklin countered, "I beg your pardon, sir. Philadelphia has taken Howe."

Inwardly, he was gravely concerned. His daughter and her family, his home, those he loved, and everything he owned was in Philadelphia. But he could not afford to let his anxiety show.

He considered at this time telling Vergennes that unless America could count on a French alliance, they would have to make terms with England, but decided the threat might boomerang and force the French to abandon them. Best wait until the news was better. It so happened he had not long to wait.

On December 4, a messenger from Boston arrived at Passy, to announce that General John Burgoyne, whom the British had sent to Canada to lead an army to invade the colonies from the north, had been defeated at Saratoga. Beaumarchais, who was present when this news came, drove off to Paris so recklessly that his carriage upset and his arm was broken.

Franklin and his two commissioners promptly drew up a dispatch for Vergennes. Two days later Conrad-Alexandre Gérard of the foreign office arrived at Passy with Vergennes' congratulations—and a request that the Americans renew their proposal for an alliance.

Franklin drafted the proposal on December 7 and Temple delivered it the next day. On the 12th, the commissioners met secretly with Vergennes. Franklin hoped the matter could be settled there and then but the French minister said France could not agree to an alliance without Spain. It took three weeks for a courier to make the trip and bring back an answer from Spain. It was negative. Temporarily negotiations were at a standstill.

In the meantime England had sent an envoy named Paul Wentworth to parley with the Americans. He passed himself off as a stock speculator though he was actually chief of the British espionage. Silas Deane saw him several times. Wentworth told him that the British ministry was ready to return to the imperial status of before 1763, suggested a general armistice with all British troops withdrawn except those on the New York islands, and added, insinuatingly, that any Americans who helped to bring about an understanding would be rewarded with wealth and titles and high administrative posts.

Franklin knew about Wentworth but refused to see him until January 6, a week after the news of Spain's rejection of the alliance. That day he conferred two hours with Wentworth, devoting the whole time to a recital of England's crimes against America. After that he and Wentworth had dinner with Silas Deane and his assistant Edward Bancroft (who was also an English spy).

The results of this dinner were exactly what Franklin anticipated. It was duly reported to Vergennes, who could only judge that negotiations for a reconciliation between England and America were under way, which was the last thing in the world he wanted. The very next day the French King's council voted formally on a treaty and an alliance with the United States of America.

The signing of the treaty took place on Friday, February 7, 1778, at the office of the ministry for foreign affairs in the Hotel de Lautrec, Paris. For this all important occasion Franklin donned an old costume, somewhat old-fashioned and rather too tight for him, of figured Manchester velvet. Someone asked him why. "To get it a little revenge," Franklin said. "I wore this coat on the day Wedderburn abused me."

The ceremony was simple. Gérard signed first, then Franklin, after which Arthur Lee and Silas Deane added their names. A magnificent diplomatic campaign had been won.

On March 20, Louis XVI avowed the treaty by receiving the three commissioners in his private quarters at Versailles. Franklin wore a brown velvet suit, white hose, and carried a white hat under his arm. He had neither wig nor sword, and his spectacles were on his nose. The courtiers claimed they had never seen anything so striking as this "republican simplicity."

To the commissioners, the King said, "Firmly assure Congress of my friendship. I hope that this will be for the good of the two nations."

Franklin responded for his fellow envoys. "Your Majesty may count on the gratitude of Congress and its faithful observance of the pledges it now takes."

That evening Vergennes gave a great dinner in their honor at Versailles. Later they made a call on the royal family. The charming and beautiful Marie Antoinette, who was at her gambling table, insisted that Franklin stand by her, and talked to him in between making her bids at exceedingly high stakes. It was certainly the first time in history that the son of an American candlemaker kept company with a queen.

15
AMERICA'S FIRST AMBASSADOR

In the spring after the signing of the treaty with France, Silas Deane was recalled to America. John Adams was sent to take his place. Franklin invited him and his wife Abigail to stay with him at Passy, and arranged for their ten-year-old son John Quincy to go to school with Benjamin Bache.

The comfortable life at Passy made Puritan-minded Adams uncomfortable. Though Franklin's taste in dress and food was exceedingly simple compared to the French aristocrats with whom he had to keep company, Adams found him extravagant. He felt it a waste of money that Arthur Lee should have separate quarters in Paris. At the same time he objected that no rent was paid at Passy and vainly tried to get Chaumont to accept payment.

He could not help himself. Basically it was simply impossible for him to approve of someone like Benjamin Franklin: "He loves his ease, hates to offend, and seldom gives any opinion till obliged to do it.... Although he has as determined a soul as any man, yet it is his constant policy never to say yes or no decidedly but when he cannot avoid it."

John Adams was a man who always said yes or no decidedly, never having, like Franklin, learned from Socrates that if you wish to convince people, making them think for themselves is more effective than bludgeoning them.

But as he was essentially honest, Adams did not deny that Franklin was beloved by the French as he would never be: "His name was familiar to government and people," he wrote later, "to king, courtiers, nobility, clergy, and philosophers, as well as plebeians, to such a degree that there was scarcely a peasant or a citizen, a *valet de chambre*, coachman or footman, a lady's chambermaid or a scullion in a kitchen who was not familiar with it and who did not consider him a friend to human kind.... When they spoke of him they seemed to think he was to restore the golden age...."

In one of the many elaborate ceremonies organized in Franklin's honor, a crown of laurel was placed on his white hair by the most beautiful of three hundred women admirers. At another, a walking stick with a gold head wrought in the form of a cap of liberty was presented to him. A poem, composed for the occasion, was read.

The wood of the cane, it said, had been seized on the plains of Marathon by the Goddess of Liberty before she abandoned Greece. It had been transported to Switzerland, where the valiant mountaineers fought against invading Austrians. More recently it had been seen at Trenton, where Washington defeated the British. By possession of this symbol of victory, Benjamin Franklin was assured of a place in the "Temple of Memory."

Franklin's French friends had long been hoping for a meeting between him and Voltaire, considered the two most enlightened men of the eighteenth century. In February 1778, after an exile of more than twenty-eight years, Voltaire returned to spend the last four months of his life in Paris. With his grandson Temple, Franklin called to pay his respects to the great philosopher. Voltaire was then eighty-four, lean and emaciated, but he still had the fiery spirit that had kept all Europe in an uproar over the major part of his life. He insisted on greeting the "illustrious and wise Franklin" in English, and held his hand over Temple's head in blessing, pronouncing the words "God and Liberty."

There was a more publicized meeting in April at the Academy of Sciences. The audience, seeing both present, clamored to have them introduced to each other. Obligingly, they stepped forward and bowed to each other. The spectators were not yet satisfied. They wanted them to embrace each other in the French manner. Only when Franklin and Voltaire put their arms around each other and kissed each other's cheeks did the tumult subside.

That year the French sculptor Jean-Antoine Houdon, who had immortalized Voltaire in marble, did his bust of Franklin, catching his likeness better than any other had done. And that Baron Turgot, the French Minister of Finance, made his most famous epigram about Franklin: "He snatched the lightning from the sky and the sceptre from the tyrants." Vainly Franklin protested that other Americans, "able and brave men," deserved credit for the Revolution.

On September 14, 1778, Congress revoked the commission of three and elected Franklin sole plenipotentiary to France—America's first official ambassador to a foreign land. With only Temple and a clerk to help him with detail work, he was in actual fact consul-general, consultant on American affairs, propagandist for America, and, the part which pleased Franklin least but which he performed expertly, official beggar to the Court of Versailles for the ever increasing sums of money which Congress instructed him to procure for their costly war.

With his other duties, he was director of naval affairs, Judge of the Admiralty, and in effect if not in name, overseas Secretary of the Navy. In this capacity in March of 1779 he wrote a "passport" for the Pacific explorer Captain James Cook, instructing commanders of American ships that Cook and his crew should be treated as "common friends to mankind" and allowed to go on their way. The sad news had not reached Europe; a month before Franklin's instructions, Cook had been killed by natives on the Hawaiian Islands.

Ever since his arrival in France, he had been concerned with the plight of captured American seamen, whom the English kept in foul prisons and treated not as prisoners-of-war but as traitors, charged with high treason and subject to execution. To Lord Stormont, the British ambassador, he had sent a formal plea requesting the exchange of American prisoners for English ones, man for man. It was ignored. A second came back unopened with a note: "The King's Ambassador receives no Letters from Rebels but when they come to implore his Majesty's Mercy."

Through an English friend, David Hartley, Franklin sent money for the relief of the American prisoners, and generous Englishmen added to the fund. That was all that could be done until some nine months after the signing of the treaty with France, when he received reluctant consent from the London ministry for prisoner exchange.

There was still the problem of getting sufficient English prisoners for the exchange. Before the treaty, British seamen on the "prizes" which American ships brought into French ports had to be set free by maritime law. With France now officially at war with England, the ban no longer applied, but there were still far fewer English prisoners in France than American ones in England.

In May 1779, as Minister of the United States at the Court of France, Franklin signed a commission for Captain Stephen Marchant of Boston, on the privateer, the *Black Prince*, to operate off the north coast of France. The *Black Prince* was so named for her sleek lines, her black sides, and her reputation as one of the swiftest vessels ever to run a cargo.

Franklin's instructions to the captain were brief and explicit. He was to bring in all the prisoners possible "to relieve so many of our countrymen from their captivity in England." He only found out later that Captain Marchant was a figurehead. The real commander of the *Black Prince* was a twenty-five-year-old Irishman named Luke Ryan, with a dazzling record as a smuggler—an honorable profession in an Ireland reduced to starvation by repressive English trade regulations.

The success of the *Black Prince* was phenomenal—twenty-nine prizes, including a recapture, in the space of two months and eleven days. Franklin gave commissions to two sister privateers, the *Black Princess* and the *Fearnot.* Their combined efforts produced a total of 114 British vessels of all descriptions, brought into free ports, burned, scuttled or ransomed. They created havoc with coastal trade in the English, Irish and Scotch seas, embarrassed the British

Admiralty, caused marine insurance rates to soar.

Franklin was proud of his three privateers and must have had a vicarious thrill in their exploits. His own role in the affair became increasingly worrisome. Each prize was judged in the local marine court of the port where it was brought. Sometimes there were delays, resulting in the loss of perishable cargo and voluble cries of protest from the crews who saw their prize money diminishing daily. In due time Franklin, as Judge of the Admiralty, received the bulky and voluminous report, handwritten and of course in French. It was up to him and Temple to appraise the contents if the venture was to be kept going.

Unfortunately, much as the privateers disrupted English shipping, the number of prisoners was far fewer than Franklin had hoped. Sometimes there was no room for prisoners on shipboard, or, when there were captive ships to man, not enough men to guard prisoners. Franklin proposed that the privateer captains get sea paroles from those they set free, but the British stubbornly refused to honor the paroles in prisoner exchange. There were also numerous British seamen who gladly joined the privateer crews, finding their free life far preferable to the cruel discipline of the British Navy.

Aside from his privateers, Franklin pinned his hope on a Scottish-born American seaman with a colorful past, named John Paul Jones. In 1778, Jones had captured the *Drake*, the first British warship to surrender to a Continental vessel. He had come to Brest from America in the *Ranger*, which had raided English and Scottish coasts, taking seven prizes. Red tape kept Jones idle for some months after that but at length he was given an aged and decrepit French forty-gun ship, which he renamed the *Bonhomme Richard*—the French translation of "Poor Richard."

In September 1779, the *Bonhomme Richard* closed in on the superior British frigate, the *Serapis*, in a battle which lasted three and a half hours. When the hull of the *Bonhomme Richard* was pierced, her decks ripped, her hold filling with water, and fires destroying her, the British captain asked if they were ready to surrender.

"Sir, I have not yet begun to fight," Jones reportedly replied.

While his ship was sinking, he and his men boarded the *Serapis* and took her captive.

Exultantly, Franklin prepared his dispatch to Congress, announcing "one of the most obstinate and bloody conflicts that has happened in this war." With even greater pleasure he reported three weeks later that John Paul Jones was safe in Texel, North Holland, with some 500 British prisoners! In Paris soon afterward the welcome given the hero of the *Bonhomme Richard* rivaled only Franklin's reception there.

At home the war was going drearily. Combined American forces failed to win Savannah from the British. A British expedition took Charleston. The British General Cornwallis, marching inland, routed General Horatio Gates. England, now at war with Holland, captured tiny St. Eustatius, thus cutting off America's chief West Indian source of supplies. Benedict Arnold had turned traitor, and the British had moved their army from Philadelphia to New York.

The Bache family, who had been living in the country, returned to find that the officers who had occupied their house had carried off some of Franklin's musical instruments, Temple's school books, and some electrical apparatus. The portrait of Franklin done by Benjamin Wilson had also vanished. It turned out that it had been taken by the English spy Major John André. (It reached England but was later restored to the White House in Washington in 1906.)

In the spring of 1781, Franklin received two American visitors at Passy, young Colonel John Laurens, son of the former Congress president Henry Laurens, and Thomas Paine. There was another financial crisis in Congress and they had come to request a loan of a million pounds sterling each year for the duration. Franklin had foreseen the need and could tell them he already had a promise of an outright gift of 6 million livres. Since July 1780, General Rochambeau and 6,000 fully equipped French regulars were in America, waiting for the auspicious time to join the conflict. France had its own to protect now.

The tide turned that year. The valiant General Nathanael Greene (nephew by marriage of Franklin's friend, Catherine Ray Greene) together with Daniel Morgan, "Light-Horse Harry" Lee, and Francis Marion (known as "The Swamp Fox") harassed Cornwallis into Virginia, where General Lafayette, in charge of his first command, forced him onto the peninsula of Yorktown. To Lafayette's aid came two armies, the American one led by Washington, and the French one led by Rochambeau. The siege lasted just nine days. Cornwallis surrendered on October 18, 1781. The news reached Franklin at eleven o'clock on the night of November 19, just one month later.

The defeat of Cornwallis at Yorktown marked the unofficial end of the war, though George III refused to believe it. In his disordered mental state, he could not face the reality of the enormous budget asked from an empty treasury. Nearly everyone else knew that the former American colonies were lost to the British Empire forever.

Franklin wrote Congress offering his resignation, planning that if it were accepted he would take his grandsons on a tour in Italy and Germany. Congress had other plans for him. Along with John Adams and John Jay of New York, he was chosen a commissioner to negotiate the formal peace with Great Britain.

"I have never known a peace made, even the most advantageous," Franklin wrote John Adams, "that was not censured as inadequate.... I esteem it, however, an honour."

John Jay and his family came to stay at Passy, as the Adams family had done. Maria Jay, age one and a half years, formed a "singular attachment" to the ancient philosopher, which he claimed he would never forget.

The peace negotiations dragged on month after month, seemingly interminable. In April 1782, in the midst of them, Franklin was stricken with a kidney stone, which disabled him the rest of his life. From then on even the jolting of his carriage over the cobblestone streets was unbearably painful. He refused either to have an operation or take drugs. "You may judge that my disease is not very grievous," he wrote John Jay, "since I am more afraid of the medicine than the malady."

The preliminary Anglo-American peace terms were finally signed on November 30, 1782, and on September 3, 1783, came the signing of the Treaty of Paris, in which Great Britain at last acknowledged the independence of the United States. The achievement of this treaty, by Franklin with John Adams and John Jay, would be labeled "the greatest triumph in the history of American diplomacy."

"May we never see another war!" wrote Franklin to Josiah Quincy. "For in my opinion there never was a good war or a bad peace."

"The times that tried men's souls are over," wrote Thomas Paine in America.

Franklin was seventy-seven, sick with gout, dropsy, and half a dozen minor ailments besides his dreadful stone, but his mind was as keen and his soul as full of fun as a youth of twenty. No one ever had a more glorious old age than he was having.

16
A GLORIOUS OLD AGE

On August 27, 1783, just a few days before the signing of the peace treaty with England, a balloon ascension was held at the Champ-de-Mars. It was the first in Paris; the first in history had taken place near Lyons in the previous June. For four days preceding the event, the great balloon of varnished silk had been filling up with hydrogen gas under the direction of the physicist Jacques-Alexandre-César Charles. Paris was agog with excitement. Some 50,000 gathered to watch.

Franklin, who was present, reported that the balloon rose rapidly "till it entered the clouds, when it seemed to me scarce bigger than an orange and soon after became invisible."

"What good is it?" a skeptic asked.

"What good is a newborn baby?" Franklin retorted, a remark that went around the world.

He saw the first free balloon ascend with human passengers on November 20, at the Château de la Muette in Passy. The passengers, scientist Pilâtre de Rozier and the Marquis d'Arland, were lifted some 500 feet, floated over the Seine, and landed in Paris. A few weeks later he witnessed a balloon soar upwards from the Paris Tuileries, taking its human cargo to the incredible height of 2,000 feet.

He could not resist speculating as to what man's triumph over space might mean to the future. Would the balloon perhaps become a common means of transportation? How delightful that would be for one like himself for whom riding in a carriage had become such agony. But he could hardly hope for such comfort in his lifetime.

More to the point was the possibility that the actuality of balloon flight might convince "sovereigns of the folly of wars":

Five thousand balloons, capable of raising two men each, could not cost more than five ships of the line; and where is the prince who can afford so to cover his country with troops for its defense as that ten thousand men descending from the clouds might not in many places do an infinite deal of mischief before a force could be brought together to repel them?

Not even the wealthiest and most powerful ruler could guard his dominions against such an air raid. The terrible threat would mean an end to warfare. So

Franklin reasoned, happily unable to peer into the future.

Following the Treaty of Paris, Congress had retained his services as ambassador to France for two years longer. He served unofficially as United States ambassador for all of Europe, and new honors rained down on him. He was elected a member of Madrid's Royal Academy of History, of Manchester's Literary and Philosophical Society, of the Academies of Sciences and Arts in the French towns of Orléans and Lyons. Through Admiral Lord Richard Howe, a staunch friend still, the British Admiralty sent him Captain Cook's *Voyage to the Pacific Ocean*, a tribute to his instructions to American cruisers to refrain from interfering with the explorer and his crew.

His real and solid pleasures came not from such tokens of recognition but from the circle of good friends he had acquired in his years at Passy. He was on good terms with the parish priest, the village tradesmen, and all the children of the town. The Chaumont family, on whose estate he lived, were deeply devoted to him, including the young daughter Sophie whom he called "my little wife."

He established strong bonds of friendship with his neighbor, the lovely and talented young Madame Brillon, wife of an elderly treasury official. For several years he called on her nearly every Wednesday and Saturday, to play chess or to idle on her terrace in the sun. Sometimes he played for her on his armonica.

Once he spent a summer day with Madame Brillon and some other companions on Moulin-Joli, an island on the Seine. Over the river hovered a swarm of tiny May flies, known as *ephemera* since their life span is but a few hours. As a souvenir of this holiday, he wrote the "Ephemera," one of his most charming fables, a delicate satire about the trivia which make up the thoughts and actions of many human souls during their own comparatively brief period on earth.

"Papa," Madame Brillon called Franklin. After she and her husband left Passy, she sent him a plaintive note. "How am I going to spend the Wednesdays and Saturdays?" Might they perhaps be united in paradise? "We shall live on roast apples only; the music will be made up of Scottish airs ... everyone will speak the same language; the English will be neither unjust nor wicked ... ambition, envy, pretensions, jealousy, prejudices, all these will vanish at the sound of the trumpet."

Young and old, French women lavished attention on the American philosopher. In return, he gave them affection both fatherly and gallant, told them amusing stories, and showed that combination of respect for their mental capacities and appreciation of their womanly charms which had won over Catherine Ray Greene so many years before.

Among his many close women friends the most celebrated was the elderly Madame Helvétius, widow of a wealthy landowner and philosopher, who lived with her two daughters at Auteuil, a village next to Passy, in the midst of a little park planted with hortensias and rhododendron, and over-run with cats, dogs, chickens, canaries, pigeons, and wild birds. "Our Lady of Auteuil," Franklin called her, while her daughters were *"les étoiles,"* the stars.

Her salon was frequented by philosophers, statesmen, poets, scientists, and mathematicians. Franklin first met her through the French minister Turgot.

When she knew him better she told him she wished she had welcomed him as she had Voltaire, whom she had greeted at her gate like a king.

One of the many scholars Franklin met at her salon was a talented young doctor named Philippe Pinel. Franklin advised him to come to America where doctors were badly needed. Pinel was tempted but refused—and became famous for his courage and wisdom in removing chains from the insane at the Paris hospitals of Bicêtre and Saltpêtrière.

While John Adams and his wife Abigail were at Passy, Franklin invited Madame Helvétius to dinner. The worthy Abigail was horrified when Madame Helvétius kissed Franklin's cheeks and forehead in greeting. Even more shocking in her eyes, the guest held Franklin's hand at dinner and now and then let her arm rest on the back of John Adams' chair.

"I should have been greatly astonished at this conduct," Abigail wrote afterwards, "if the good Doctor had not told me that in this lady I should see a genuine Frenchwoman, wholly free from affectation or stiffness of behaviour, and one of the best women in the world. For this I must take the Doctor's word; but I should have set her down for a very bad one."

Whatever Abigail Adams thought, there is no doubt of Franklin's devotion. Sometime—no one knows just when—he proposed marriage to Madame Helvétius. She refused him. Perhaps she was too accustomed to her own way of life to want to make a change. Perhaps she felt that his proposal was only a form of gallantry. Neither the proposal nor her refusal interfered with their friendship, which lasted as long as he stayed in France and by correspondence afterward.

Since 1777 he had his own private press at Passy and a foundry to cast his own type. His excuse was that the press was useful with so many official forms to be prepared, but it was also true that printing was still in his blood and always would be.

One of the pamphlets that came off the Passy printing press was "Information to Those who would Remove to America." He thought too many of the wrong people wanted to emigrate to America for the wrong reasons, and he wanted to correct their misapprehensions. He discouraged artists and scholars who expected they would receive free transportation, land, slaves, tools and livestock from a rich but ignorant America. In America, a man who did not bring his fortune "must work and be industrious to live."

The chief resource of America was cheap land, he pointed out. Farm laborers were needed. Skilled artisans could make a good living and "provide for children and old age." But "those Europeans who have these or greater advantages at home would do well to stay where they are."

To answer those who besieged him with questions about the Indians, he wrote "Remarks Concerning the Savages of North America," perhaps the first fair appraisal of America's original inhabitants to be printed:

The Indian men, when young, are hunters and warriors; when old, counsellors; for all their government is by counsel of the sages; there is no force, there are no prisons, no officers to compel obedience or inflict punishment.... The Indian women till the ground, dress the food, nurse and bring up the children, and preserve and hand down to posterity the memory of public transactions. These employments of men and women are accounted natural and honourable. Having few artificial wants they have abundance of leisure for improvement by conversation. Our laborious manner of life, compared with theirs, they esteem slavish and base; and the learning on which we value ourselves they regard as frivolous and useless....

So he continued, by illustration and by example, to show that while Indian ways and customs were quite different from those of the white men, there was much to be said for them, and they were by no means always inferior. In fact, there was much which men who called themselves civilized could learn by studying the nature of those called savages.

Some pieces in lighter vein were also run off his press, which Franklin wrote partly as an exercise in French, partly to entertain himself and his friends. In one of these bagatelles, as such pieces are known, he told Parisians of a discovery he had made whereby they could make great savings in the cost of candles and oil lamps. He had gone to bed one night, as usual at three or four hours after midnight, and had been awakened by a sudden noise at six, to find that his room was flooded with light! His servant had forgotten to close the shutters before he retired. Looking into his almanac, he learned what few others could know—that the sun rises early and *"that he gives light as soon as he rises."*

Another of his bagatelles was "Dialogue between Franklin and the Gout," in which Gout explains his frequent and unwelcome visits as due simply to Franklin's indolence; he plays chess too much and exercises too little. The "Ephemera" was printed as a bagatelle, and so was "The Whistle," an expanded version of the little story he had once told his son William.

His intellectual curiosity had not slackened during his years in France. War or no war, he continued to observe natural phenomenon, write and reflect on scientific matters, and keep up with the newest discoveries and inventions.

He attended meetings of the Royal Society of Medicine, to which he had been elected in 1777, and of the French Academy of Science. In 1782, he watched Antoine-Laurent Lavoisier perform an experiment with the gas he had named oxygen—Joseph Priestley's "dephlogistated air." He wrote to Jan Ingenhousz, a Dutch scientist, about differences between the Leyden jar and Volta's new electrophorus, and to Edward Nairne, an English friend, about the comparative humidity of the air in London, Philadelphia and Passy.

To a French friend, Count de Gebelin, he discoursed on the characteristics of the various Indian languages. When de Gebelin commented that some Indian words sounded Phoenician, Franklin dived into archaeological speculations:

If any Phoenicians arrived in America, I should rather think it was not by the accident of a storm but in the course of their long and adventurous voyages; and that they coasted from Denmark and Norway over to Greenland, and down southward by Newfoundland, Nova Scotia, etc., to New England; as the Danes themselves certainly did some ages before Columbus.

He wrote a paper on the phenomenon of the aurora borealis (the northern lights) for the French Academy of Science, sent notes to Marie Antoinette's physician, Felix Vicq d'Azyr, on the length of time infection could remain in the body after death, and investigated a story of some workmen in the Passy quarry who claimed to have found living toads shut up in solid stone.

In a letter to another friend, the Abbé Soulavie, he pondered on why there were coal mines under the sea at Whitehaven and oyster shells in the Derbyshire mountains—indications of great geological changes in the past. Was it possible that the surface of the earth was a shell "capable of being broken and disordered by the violent movements of the fluid on which it rested?" Admittedly, this was only a guess: "I approve much more your method of philosophizing, which proceeds upon actual observations...."

He still tinkered with inventions, and for his own comfort devised the first bifocal glasses, so he could see both near and far without changing his spectacles.

He was old enough to be serious all the time, but he never could resist a hoax, even with his scientific friends. To the eminent French physician Georges Cabanis he confided that in the forests of North America he had observed a bird which "like the horned screamer or the horned lapwing, carries two horned tubercles at the joints of the wings. These two tubercles at the death of the bird become the sprouts of two vegetable stalks, which grow at first in sucking the juice from its cadaver and which subsequently attach themselves to the earth in order to live in the manner of plants and trees."

The inspiration for this weird creation of his imagination was perhaps the "vegetable animal" he thought he saw on the gulf weed he had fished out of the Gulf Stream at the age of twenty. His friend Cabanis, suspecting nothing, dutifully reported it in one of his books, taking only the precaution to note that "in spite of the great veracity of Franklin, I cite it with a great deal of reserve."

What endless marvels the world offered and how much there was to know about them! One lifetime was not nearly long enough. "The rapid progress true science now makes occasions my regretting sometimes that I was born so soon," he wrote Joseph Priestley after their countries were at peace once more. "It is impossible to imagine the height to which may be carried, in a thousand years, the power of man over matter.... O that moral science were in as fair a way of improvement that men would cease to be wolves to one another, and that human beings would at length learn what they now improperly call humanity." He could not guess that his fervent cry would still be echoed, in one form or another, more than a hundred and seventy-five years after his death.

In 1784, the King of France chose him to serve on a commission of five to investigate the work of Dr. Franz Anton Mesmer, who claimed to effect cures through "animal magnetism,"—a universal fluid which flowed to his patients from the healer, or from some object "magnetized" by the healer, such as a tree. All fashionable Paris was flocking to Mesmer's seances; his following was enormous throughout France.

With Franklin on this commission served Joseph-Ignace Guillotin (whose name would survive in the French Revolution's chief instrument of execution) and the scientist Lavoisier (whom the guillotine would claim as a victim). After many months of study, the commission concluded that "animal magnetism" did not exist, and that Mesmer's cures were the result of "imagination." The importance of imagination in physical illness was as yet unrecognized. Privately Franklin commented that Mesmer's treatments certainly did some good—at least they kept some from taking injurious drugs.

On the whole the findings of the commission brought both Mesmer and mesmerism into disrepute. Indirectly the shadow of its disapproval fell on a phenomenon first discovered by a Mesmer disciple, the Marquis de Puysegur—that some persons, in a state of trance and apparently asleep, are able to obey simple commands. Hypnotism, for many years after de Puysegur's observations, was relegated to quacks rather than physicians and scientists.

In August of 1784 Thomas Jefferson arrived from America to help negotiate treaties with European and North African powers. Franklin introduced him to his French scientific friends and found in his company the same harmony as when they were both members of the Second Continental Congress. His last winter in France, Polly Hewson and her children also joined him at Passy. Mrs. Stevenson, Polly's mother, had died in England during the war. Franklin welcomed these members of his "English family" with joy and affection.

He still had his two grandsons with him. There had been some objections from Congress to his making Temple his secretary, on the grounds that he was the son of a traitor. Franklin had been highly indignant: "Methinks it is rather some merit that I have rescued a valuable young man from the danger of being a Tory, and fixed him in honest republican Whig principles."

Yet there was some justification in the fears of Congress. At twenty-six, Temple was charming, handsome and spoiled. He spent his evenings at music halls and, wearing red heels, an embroidered coat, and with an Angora cat on a leash, paraded the boulevards with aristocratic young friends. Mockingly the Parisians dubbed him "Franklinet." While Franklin was trying to kill a clause in the peace treaty conceding special privileges to Tories, Temple, without his knowledge, wrote to Lord Shelburne pleading a government post for his Tory father.

Different as could be was Benjamin Bache, now sixteen, a husky wholesome youngster much like Franklin at his age.

He wanted no more than to be a printer as his grandfather had been. Franklin taught him how to cast type, and in April 1785 persuaded the best printer in France to make him an apprentice. The arrangement was of short duration.

In May, Franklin at last received permission from Congress to come home. Jefferson was appointed ambassador to France in his stead. "I am not replacing Franklin," Jefferson said loyally. "No one could do that. I am only his successor."

He left Passy on July 12, 1785, traveling to Havre in a royal litter drawn by mules, which the King had provided for his comfort. His personal goods—128 boxes in all—went by barge down the Seine. He took with him Louis XVI's personal gift— the King's miniature, set with 408 diamonds. The whole population of Passy watched him leave, silent except for occasional outbursts of sobs.

"All the days of my life I shall remember that a great man, a sage, wished to be my friend," wrote Madame Brillon just before his departure. A farewell note from Madame Helvétius was waiting for him at Havre: "I see you in your litter, every step taking you further from us, lost to me and all my friends who love you so much and to whom you leave such long regrets."

He and his grandsons spent four days at Southampton, England. William Franklin came down from London, where he was now living, to see them, but the meeting with his father was brief and strained. Then Benjamin Franklin set off for his eighth crossing of the Atlantic. He knew it would be his last.

17
THE CLOSING YEARS

Never had America given a returning hero a more resounding welcome. Booming cannons announced his landing on September 14, 1785, at Philadelphia's Market Street wharf. Bells rang throughout the city and the whole town was out to greet him. Cheering crowds lined the street as his carriage proceeded to his home at Franklin Court, where Sally and his grandchildren, eight now in all, were waiting for him. Ceremonies in his honor continued for weeks.

Old and feeble and almost constantly in pain, he was still not allowed to relax. On October 11, he was made president of the Supreme Executive Council of the

Pennsylvania Assembly—an Assembly which would never again have to pay heed to "the proprietors." On October 29, two weeks later, he was elected president of Pennsylvania. To avoid the agony of riding in a carriage, he had a sedan chair built, so he could be carried to meetings.

His eightieth birthday, January 6, 1786, was celebrated at the Bunch of Grapes Tavern by Philadelphia's now numerous printers. They drank their first toast to their "venerable printer, philosopher, and statesman." At least once in this period George Washington came to dinner with him. One pleasant afternoon and evening he spent with Thomas Paine, now one of America's most distinguished citizens; together they worked on inventing a "smokeless candle." For a while, Franklin kept in his garden a model of an iron bridge which Paine had invented and which attracted droves of curious visitors.

He tried vainly to secure a post for Temple, but Congress was still doubtful about him. Later he bought the young man a farm at Rancocas, New Jersey. Temple liked farm life so little he spent most of his time in Philadelphia. For Benjamin Bache he set up a printing press and type foundry, which the youth managed contentedly until at the age of thirty an attack of yellow fever brought his life to a premature end.

In July 1786, an Indian chief of the Wyandots, named Scotosh, came to Franklin with a message from his people, bringing strings of white wampum. Franklin received him with the same courtesy due any ambassador. Following the Indian custom, he waited two days to consider the chief's message, then presented more strings of wampum with his reply.

In the Pennsylvania Assembly, that September, he helped revise the penal code. No longer were men to be hanged for robbery, arson, or counterfeiting. By the new act only murder and treason warranted capital punishment. Branding with a hot iron, flogging, the pillory were all abolished. Such barbarities did not belong in a new nation.

He was pleased with signs of progress and quick recovery from war. "Our working-people are all employed and get high wages, are well fed and well clad," he wrote in November. "Buildings in Philadelphia increase rapidly, besides small towns rising in every quarter of the country. The laws govern, justice is well administered, and property is as secure as in any country in the globe.... In short, all among us may be happy who have happy dispositions; such being necessary to happiness even in paradise."

But all was not yet honey and roses in the new United States, as he soon discovered. Much trouble had risen because of the lack of power of the Confederacy.

Under the Articles of the Confederation, Congress might declare war, but could not enlist a single soldier. Congress could ask the states for money, but had no authority to raise a dollar by taxation. It could make treaties but could not force the states to recognize them. It could not regulate commerce and each state taxed imports as it wished. Not only the Confederacy, but all the states issued their own money, resulting in endless confusion.

To create a strong central government, the Constitutional Convention opened on May 25, 1787, at the Philadelphia State House, in the same room where the

Declaration of Independence had been signed. Franklin, who was the oldest delegate here, as he had been at the Second Continental Congress, expressed the hope that good would come from the Convention: "Indeed if it does not do good it must do harm, as it will show that we have not wisdom enough among us to govern ourselves."

There were fifty-five delegates in all, the best minds in America. George Washington was the natural choice as presiding officer. All that hot summer they labored on the task of making a workable constitution.

Franklin did not miss a meeting in the four months. As always, he said little. When he had a speech to make, he wrote it out in advance and let James Wilson, or some other delegate, read it for him. He could no longer stand to deliver an address without pain. In the course of the sessions he advocated three ideas—a single legislature, a plural executive, the nonpayment of officers. All three were rejected. He accepted the defeat without rancor.

His main role was as a peacemaker. In case of an impasse, as was inevitable with so many contrary views and opinions, it was invariably he who suggested a workable compromise. Once, when feelings were taut to the point of hostility, he moved that the Convention open its sessions with prayer:

"I have lived a long time, and the longer I live the more convincing proofs I see of this truth: that God governs in the affairs of men. And if a sparrow cannot fall to the ground without His notice, is it probable that an empire can rise without His aid?"

His motion was received with respect but no action was taken on it. Perhaps he guessed there would be none. Whether he planned it or not, his proposal had the effect of cooling hot tempers, and work continued with less dissension.

The final day of the Convention was Monday, September 17. The great document, which was the fruit of their heavy labor, was read by the secretary. Then James Wilson gave Franklin's comments:

I confess that there are several parts of this Constitution which I do not at present approve, but I am not sure I shall never approve them; for, having lived long, I have experienced many instances of being obliged by better information or fuller consideration to change my opinions.... In these sentiments, sir, I agree to this Constitution with all its faults, if there are such; because I think a general government necessary for us, and there is no form of government but what may be a blessing to the people if well administered.... Thus I consent, sir, to this Constitution because I expect no better, and because I am not sure that it is not the best....

Then Franklin moved that the Constitution be signed by the delegates as "done in Convention by the unanimous consent of the states present."

While the last delegates were affixing their signature, Franklin's eyes were on the president's chair, on the back of which a sunset—or sunrise—was painted. To those near him he said, "I have often and often in the course of the session ... looked at that sun behind the president without being able to tell whether it was rising or setting. But now at length I have the happiness to know that it is a rising and not a setting sun."

In the year of the Convention, the Massachusetts delegate, Elbridge Gerry, called on Franklin, bringing a friend named Manasseh Cutler. Later Cutler wrote down his recollections of this first meeting with the philosopher-statesman.

He was sitting hatless under a mulberry tree in his garden, "a short, fat, trunched old man in a plain Quaker dress, bald pate, and short white locks." Present were several men and women, one of whom was Sarah Bache. When Cutler was introduced, Franklin rose, took him by the hand, expressed his joy at seeing him, and begged him to be seated by his side. He spoke in a low voice and his "countenance was open, frank, and pleasing."

Sarah Bache served tea under the tree. She had three of her younger children with her, who "seemed to be excessively fond of their grandpapa." They talked until dark when Franklin took his guests into his study, "a very large chamber and high-studded." The walls were lined with bookshelves and there were more books in four alcoves extending two-thirds of the length of the room. Cutler guessed rightly that this was "the largest and by far the best private library in America."

Their host showed them a sort of artificial arm—a long pole with prongs at the end that could be opened or shut with a rope, which he had devised to take down and put up books on the upper shelves. (Previously he had used a chair which could be unfolded into a ladder, but now he was not sufficiently agile.) He had other curiosities in the room, such as a glass machine for "exhibiting the circulation of the blood in the arteries and veins of the human body" and his rocking armchair, with a fan placed over it which he could operate by a small motion of his foot.

Because Cutler was a botanist, Franklin showed him a precious folio containing *Systema Vegetabilium*, by Linnaeus, the founder of systematic botany. Heavy as the folio was, Franklin insisted on lifting it himself, and to Cutler he expressed regret that he had not in his youth given more attention to the science of botany.

They discussed many other matters and Cutler was astonished at Franklin's extensive knowledge, "the brightness of his memory, and clearness and vivacity of all his mental faculties, notwithstanding his age," and at the "incessant vein of humour ... which seems as natural and involuntary as his breathing."

But his age was catching up with Benjamin Franklin, as no one realized better than he. In February 1788, he fell on the stone steps that led into his garden, bruising himself badly and spraining his wrist, so that temporarily he could not even write to his friends. The accident was followed by a severe attack of his kidney stone ailment. He was still confined to bed when Pennsylvania celebrated gloriously its twelfth Fourth of July. The Pennsylvania Council held meetings at his house during his illness, and in October, Thomas Mifflin, a veteran of the Revolutionary War, was elected to succeed him.

To quiet the anxiety of his sister in Boston, Jane Mecom, he wrote, "There are in life real evils enough, and it is a folly to afflict ourselves with imaginary ones.... As to the pain I suffer, about which you make yourself so unhappy, it is, when compared with the long life I have enjoyed of health and ease, but a trifle."

He made his will that summer of 1788. In a codicil, he bequeathed to "my friend, and the friend of mankind, General

Washington," the walking stick with the gold head in the shape of a cap of liberty, which had been given him in France as a symbol of victory.

Congress was now allotting many pensions and bonuses to patriots who had sacrificed their personal interests to serve in the cause of freedom. Franklin had hoped that his many years of foreign service might be thought worthy of a grant of a tract of land in the West "which might have been of some use and some honour to my posterity." This was never given him.

Arthur Lee, who had been notably jealous of Franklin and who had written him vitriolic letters in France accusing him of leaving him out of things, was a member of the Treasury Board. He had never forgotten or forgiven Franklin for being the better man. John Adams was finding ears to listen to his long-standing disapproval of Franklin's "frivolity." He was being criticized for being too fond of France, as he had once been censored for his attachment to England, and especially for accepting as a gift the King of France's miniature. There was also a matter of a million livres given by France to the dummy importing concern, Hortalez and Company, which was unaccounted for. Franklin was condemned by innuendo, though time would clear him completely.

He was sorrowful about this turn of affairs but he blamed nobody. He knew something of the "nature of such changeable assemblies," he wrote a friend, "and how little successors are informed of services that have been rendered to the corps before their admission."

Once more he had turned to working on his *Autobiography*, commenced years before at the Shipley home in England. For six months off and on he kept at it, even while his kidney stone was causing him such acute pain he had to resort to opium. He brought his life story up to the time of his first meetings with the Penn brothers in England. It remained unfinished.

By the summer of 1789 he was so emaciated that, in his words, "little remains of me but a skeleton covered with a skin," and philosophic as always, commented, "In this world, nothing can be said to be certain except death and taxes," tossing off another epigram that would survive.

The long fermenting discontent of the French working classes exploded in the storming of the Bastille on July 14, 1789. Franklin seems not to have realized the extent of the misery in France during his stay there. Most of his intimate friends had been wealthy, or at least well-to-do. His own life had been so idyllic he had come to think of his foster country almost as a utopia. Moreover, he was deeply grateful to the French King for his generosity to America.

But his belief in the rights of the common man was firm and if the people of France felt they needed a change, he was with them. When rumors of their Revolution reached him, he wrote, "Disagreeable circumstances might attend the convulsions in France ... but if by the struggle she obtains and secures for her nation its future liberty, and a good constitution, a few years' enjoyment of those blessings will amply repair all the damages their acquisition may have occasioned."

Since 1787 he had been president of the Pennsylvania Society for Promoting the

Abolition of Slavery, founded by the Quakers, and his signature was on a memorial which the society sent to Congress on February 12, 1790, advocating the abolition of slavery. Congress dismissed the memorial on the grounds that it had no authority to interfere in the internal affairs of the states. Whereupon Franklin promptly published an essay, "On the Slave Trade," in which a mythical Algerian, Sidi Mehemet Ibrahim, used the same arguments as the Negro slave owners to defend his right to Christian slaves! The piece showed the same barbs of wit and satire as his earlier writings. His campaign against slavery was his last public activity.

His pain now kept him bedridden, but he did some work, using Benjamin Bache as his secretary, and he found the energy to listen to his nine-year-old granddaughter Deborah recite lessons from her Webster spelling book. In March, Thomas Jefferson, on his way to accept his post as Secretary of State under President George Washington, came to see him, and on April 8, he wrote Jefferson his last letter, a clear account of the map which he and the other peace commissioners used in fixing the boundary between Maine and Nova Scotia.

He was now running a high temperature. Breathing became so difficult that he nearly suffocated. When, briefly, he felt a little better, he rose from his bed, begging that it might be made up fresh for him so he could die in a decent manner.

His daughter Sally told him she hoped he would recover and live many years longer.

"I hope not," he said calmly.

They put him back to bed and his physician advised him to change his position so he could breathe more easily.

"A dying man can do nothing easy," he commented.

Soon afterwards he fell in a coma. Temple and Benjamin Bache, his grandsons, were alone with him when, on April 17, 1790, at the age of eighty-four and three months, the end came.

His death brought an abrupt halt to the petty recriminations that had saddened his last months. In Philadelphia, the city that had grown up with him and because of him, muffled bells tolled, and flags on the ships in the harbor hung at half mast. Some 20,000 attended his funeral, the greatest number the city had ever seen gathered in one spot. As he was lowered into his grave in the Christ Church burying ground beside his wife, a company of militia artillery fired funeral guns in honor of the man who had organized Pennsylvania's first militia.

In New York, by a motion passed unanimously, the United States House of Representatives voted to wear mourning for a month. Neither the Senate nor the Executive Council followed the example of the House. Ironically, the man chosen to pronounce his funeral eulogy at the Lutheran German Church in Philadelphia was William Smith, his ancient enemy. Although Smith did not do him justice, the crowd before the pulpit sobbed openly.

But it was in France, his adopted country, where the expressions of grief and loss were most tumultuous. The National Assembly proclaimed a period of three months of national mourning for the "benefactor and hero of humanity." "Antiquity would have raised altars to this mighty genius," cried the revolutionary leader Mirabeau.

Splendid orations in his honor were delivered by the Jacobins, the Friends of the Constitution, the Academy of Science, the Royal Society of Medicine, the National Guard, the Masonic lodges, the printers of France, and uncounted other societies. All over the country, women wept for him. It is said that one enterprising businessman became rich by selling statuettes of him, made from the stones of the Bastille.

Franklin's contributions to his country, to science, to better understanding between nations and peoples were immense. His maxims on thrift and moral virtues have been extolled to generations of school children. His wit and wisdom have added to the world's riches. He was many men in one—statesman, scientist, inventor, writer, humorist, philosopher, and a friend of humanity who shared himself with all around him.

"Who that know and love you can bear the thoughts of surviving you in this gloomy world?" cried out Jane Mecom, his beloved sister, shortly before his death.

Posterity would provide her answer. Because Benjamin Franklin lived and enjoyed life, the world would be a little less gloomy and a little more pleasant for all who came after him.

SOMMARIO

BENJAMIN FRANKLIN 1

1   A BOYHOOD IN BOSTON 2

2   A YOUNG MAN ON HIS OWN 21

3   THE BIRTH OF POOR RICHARD 42

4   THE CIVIC-MINDED CITIZEN 63

5   THE THUNDER GIANT 85

6   A BRIEF MILITARY CAREER 111

7   THE BATTLE WITH THE PENNS .. 135

8   THE WHITE CHRISTIAN SAVAGES 156

9   THE STAMP ACT 170

10   FRIENDSHIPS IN ENGLAND 188

11 THE TERRIBLE HUTCHINSON LETTERS................. 210

12 BEGINNING OF A LONG WAR 234

13 THE SPLENDID WORD INDEPENDENCE 253

14 FRANCE FALLS IN LOVE WITH AN AMERICAN................................. 275

15 AMERICA'S FIRST AMBASSADOR 299

16 A GLORIOUS OLD AGE.................. 319

17 THE CLOSING YEARS 343

THE AUTHOR 370

BENJAMIN FRANKLIN..................... 371

SUGGESTED READING

Aldrich, Alfred Owen, *Franklin and His French Contemporaries.* New York, New York University Press, 1957.

The American Heritage Book of the Revolution. By the Editors of American Heritage. New York, Simon & Schuster, 1958.

Augur, Helen, *The Secret War of Independence.* New York, Duell, Sloan and Pearce, 1955.

Burt, Struthers, *Philadelphia Holy Experiment.* New York, Doubleday & Company, Inc., 1945.

Clark, William Bell, *Ben Franklin's Privateers.* Baton Rouge, La., Louisiana State University Press, 1956.

Fäy, Bernard, *Franklin, the Apostle of Modern Times*. Boston, Little, Brown, and Company, 1929.

Ford, Paul Leicester, *The Many-Sided Franklin*. New York, The Century Company, 1899.

Franklin's Wit & Folly—the Bagatelles, edited by Richard E. Amacher. New Brunswick, N.J., Rutgers University Press, 1953.

A Benjamin Franklin Reader, edited by Nathan G. Goodman. New York, Thomas Y. Crowell Company, 1945.

Benjamin Franklin's Autobiographical Writings, selected and edited by Carl Van Doren. New York, The Viking Press, 1945.

The Autobiography of Benjamin Franklin, with postcript by Richard B. Morris. New York, The Pocket Library, 1954.

Van Doren, Carl, *Benjamin Franklin*. New York, The Viking Press, 1938.

Van Doren, Carl, *Jane Mecom*. New York, The Viking Press, 1950.

THE AUTHOR

Robin McKown was born in Denver and attended the University of Colorado, Northwestern University, and the University of Illinois. She sold her first one-act play to a literary magazine while she was still in college, and later won a drama prize at the University of Colorado. She has worked in public relations, with a literary agency, and prepared radio scripts. Mrs. McKown is the author of *Thomas Paine* and *Marie Curie*, both in the Lives to Remember series, as well as

Publicity Girl and *Foreign Service Girl*. She makes her home in New York City.

BENJAMIN FRANKLIN

Few men have more claims to greatness than Benjamin Franklin. He was in his long lifetime, writer, editor and publisher, scientist and inventor, propagandist for the cause of the American colonies, statesman, diplomat. He was a wit and a humorist, a loyal friend and a good family man. From his birth in Boston as the son of a poor candlemaker to his election by Congress as America's first ambassador to France and his subsequent return to the United States, the author traces the fascinating development of an impetuous and saucy youth who became a beloved man both on his native soil and throughout the world.

Made in the USA
Monee, IL
08 March 2021